Into the Sunlight

OTHER BOOKS
BY ROGER RAPOPORT

Is the Library Burning
(with Laurence J. Kirshbaum)

The Great American Bomb Machine

The Superdoctors

The Big Player
(with Kenneth S. Uston)

The California Catalogue
(with Margot Lind)

*California Dreaming:
the Political Odyssey of Pat and Jerry Brown*

22 Days in California

22 Days in Asia
(with Burl Willes)

22 Days in the Rockies

22 Days Around the World
(with Burl Willes)

Into the *Sunlight*

Life after the Iron Curtain

by Roger Rapoport

Heyday Books, Berkeley, California

In memory of my mother,
who was nearly always ahead of her time

Heyday Books
P.O. Box 9145
Berkeley, CA 94709
415-549-3564

Book Design: Alison Wong
Typesetting: Lindsay Mugglestone
Photography:
    Antonin Novy: front cover, pp. 3, 32
    Roger Rapoport: pp. 6, 8, 9, 13, 15, 16, 21, 23, 35, 49,
    62, 73, 85, 87, 89, 92, 94, 95, 97
    Interpress Warsaw: p. 10
    Hansjoerg Krauss: pp. 26, 29, 67
    John Lee: pp. 41, 43, 46, 51, 53, 59, 81, 83
    William Feaster: p.57
    Steve Hotvedt: back cover

Illustration on p. 75 courtesy of Next Gallery,
    Berkeley, California

Library of Congress Catalogue Card Number 90-085792
ISBN 0-930588-49-5
Printed in the United States of America by
Spilman Printing, Sacramento, California

Table of Contents

Acknowledgments

M any friends and colleagues helped make this book possible. I want to thank Roy Aarons, Peter Beren, Tracey Broderick, Tom Duncan, Dennis Dutton, Calvin Goodman, Tom Faupl, Leslie Henriques, Steve Hotvedt, Steve Kearsley, Diana Ketcham, Robert and Nancy Maynard, Mark McGonigle, Lindsay Mugglestone, Ray Riegert, Victoria Shoemaker, Peter Tannenbaum, Belinda Taylor, Burl Willes, Alison Wong, and Dorothy Yule.

In Europe and the Soviet Union Alexander Bessmertnyi, Sergei Ivanov, Evelyn Miksch, Antonin Novy, Renata Jachimek, Miroslav Jirsak, Andrea Rybarova, Ernst Sucharipa, Brigitte Timmerman, Katarina Von Ledersteger, and Ewa Wowczak were all helpful. And a tip of the hat to my publisher Malcolm Margolin and Bob Drews who edited this manuscript.

The editors of the *Oakland Tribune*, where some of this material first appeared in different form, deserve special thanks. I also appreciate the assistance of the staff of Ulysses Press and the Heart to Heart team.

Introduction

I'll never forget the night the Communist Party died in Poland. Downtown Warsaw was cold and quiet, a dimly lit city short on nightlife. There I was, an eyewitness to history, and, as far as I could tell, the only non-Communist staying at Warsaw's Grand Hotel. All their waking hours were spent inside the Palace of Culture administering the last rites at the final Communist Party congress. Business was so slow at the Grand that the bar shut down at 7 p.m. and the glum hookers were reduced to propositioning reporters.

A little frightened by their brazen attitude ("What is your room number?"), I put the chain lock on my door and flicked on the television to catch the live coverage of this Bolshevik cortege. Events were moving so fast in Eastern Europe, I concluded, that it was only a matter of time until Moscow started trying to protect what was left of its empire by running prime time skin flicks and giving away banned 19th-century history books via telephone in TV lotteries to keep pro-democracy protestors off the streets. Such programming certainly would have been a step up from the wake being televised that night in my Warsaw hotel room.

Who would have believed that the Communist Party in Poland—and across Eastern Europe—would have died such a swift death? Who would have believed that Lithuanians would stand up to their Soviet masters after more than 40 years in Moscow's shadow? Who would have believed that the Soviet people—taught

that Americans and their way of life were their mortal enemy—
would be queuing up to buy Big Macs?

By now, believe it we must as political changes sweep across
Europe with bewildering speed, and in the process alter the way
Americans look at people we have been taught to fear since the end
of World War II. Beyond these winds of change is something more
basic—millions of people, blinking, seeing freedom of religion,
politics and economics for the first time in decades. Like us, these
people have the same aspirations of the good life, the same dreams
of being guided by their conscience rather than by the state. Their
frustrations with a centralized existence, their reactions to a
suddenly unshackled life are the same as ours would be. To read
about them is to read about us.

These chapters are a collection of incidents, experiences and
conversations with Eastern Europeans and Soviets I gathered during
a visit to this region in January and February of 1990. They give a
glimpse into daily life beyond the now-tattered Iron Curtain. As that
curtain was torn to shreds, so surely will our conception of what
people and life there are like. Now free to elect their own leaders,
worship as they see fit, publish the newspapers they want and
compete openly with state businesses, some Eastern Europeans
assert they are freer than Americans who need big money or
connections to it to succeed in national politics.

When was the last time a playwright or a union leader was a
leading political figure in this country? When have Americans, as the
Poles are now doing, ever said they were willing to sacrifice the
material world to pay off the debts of past regimes? And has there
ever been a time in our history, as is happening across Eastern
Europe, where elected leaders have systematically refused to accept
the traditional perks of high office?

The significance of this revolt transcends the special interests
of both the Communists and the Western powers. This is not simply
the story of an attempt to convert failed command economies into
market-driven systems of production and distribution. Nor should
we expect these newly liberated nations of Eastern Europe to
become wards of the Western superpowers standing in line for
foreign aid. Now that they have gained the right of self deter-

Czech boy celebrates the 1989 revolution with a picture
of Alexander Dubcek, hero of Prague Spring, 1968

mination, look for these countries to find creative solutions to the
crises created by Communism. Look for them to come up with
promising new ideas in politics, economics, social welfare and
education.

Read about these people, think about them as they take their
first halting steps into life as we know it.

My trip had its genesis in the summer of 1989 with an
invitation to join a group of Oakland doctors on an October trip to
Leningrad. My plan was to visit Eastern Europe and then join the

medical group in the Soviet Union. But a hospital strike in Oakland forced a postponement and all fall I watched from afar as the political crisis began to reach a critical mass.

In October, East German Prime Minister Erich Honecker was dismissed and indicted for treason. Days after Honecker was deposed, Hungary established its independence from the Soviets by proclaiming a new republic. Two weeks later the Berlin Wall fell, and the next day Bulgarian Communist strongman Todor Zhivkov was looking for work. By December, Gustav Husak, Moscow's man in Prague, had stepped down, and former jailbird and playwright Vaclav Havel celebrated his new regime by giving all the money for his inaugural ball to impoverished Romania. A new government in that country had just executed the ultimate cold warriors, the Ceausescus, the couple that conserved on energy by eliminating home heating for their citizens in the dead of winter. And this was only a partial list.

Finally, in mid-January, I set off for Vienna, seat of the Hapsburgs, the first of three empires that ruled Eastern Europe during this century. Landing in Austria, I read a story about a previous day's pro-democracy protest against the Communist regime in Mongolia where the wind chill factor was minus 80°. The whole thing was beginning to sound like a fantasy script by the late Senator Joseph McCarthy with special effects by J. Edgar Hoover.

1

Communism R.I.P.

This was the first time I'd seen anyone picket a funeral. What had started out as a rally on the steps of the Palace of Culture as the Communists met inside had been pushed across the street to the Warsaw train depot. Twenty-seven-year-old Peter Gagorny told me he had shown up to simply heap some dirt on the Communist corpse: "This is the first time in my life that Poland is free. We want to be sure that the Communists never return. That is our nightmare." An older woman on his right was quick to add: "It will take years for the new Solidarity-led government to correct all the mistakes they made, to recover from the economic crisis they created for Poland."

Before she could elaborate, the police, with batons and blue shields raised, were charging in our direction to disperse the crowd. Within seconds everyone around me had fled into the Warsaw night.

The Poles, like many other Eastern Europeans, are fiercely independent. After hundreds of years under the thumb of Vienna's Hapsburgs, the devastation of Hitler's stormtroopers and 45 years of the Moscow morning line, the Poles want independence even if it means making their own mistakes. The morning after the Communist Party died, listen to Zygmunt Gzyra in his downtown Warsaw Ministry of Finance office.

"Right now we are going through a very difficult period of change, kind of like the transition from feudalism to capitalism. Our

"We've gradually been able to convince people who need help that it's honorable to eat for free." —Zygmunt Gzyra

society is prepared to pay the cost that includes our $40 billion national debt to the world.

"Today the Warsaw Philharmonic, actors, pop musicians and artists are all staging special events and telethons to help raise money to pay this national debt. Retired people are chipping in despite our inflation problem. So far we've raised over 4 billion zlotys (more than $400,000). Students in Cracow are also donating time to renovate universities and even do medical translation to help our struggling hospitals. One of our problems is introducing the concept of charity. People weren't sure it was right to use Warsaw's 50 new soup kitchens. But we've gradually been able to convince people who need help that it's honorable to eat for free."

Materialism, the focus of Karl Marx's critique of the capitalist state, is central to the independence movement. Boris Yeltsin, Gorbachev's best-known political critic in the Soviet Union and head of the Russian Republic, likes to say that Communism only works for a couple of dozen people, namely the top leaders who can help themselves to all the consumer spoils denied the proletariat. And in the process of subsidizing themselves, state industries, food, housing, medical care and other social programs, the Poles ran up a $40 billion debt.

The immediate impact of Poland's march toward democracy is the introduction of such inspiring features of capitalism as unemployment insurance in a country that had no joblessness for 40 years. Yet the people have faith that their economic prospects will improve. Layoffs, a new word in the Polish vocabulary, are seen as the inevitable cost of joining the Western economy, attracting major foreign investment and making the zloty convertible to hard Western currencies like dollars or marks.

Rather than subsidize inefficient state industries with generous lines of credit, Warsaw is now forcing them to compete on the free market. Although consumer prices have doubled since the end of the Communist regime, most Poles voice faith in Finance Minister Leszek Balcerowicz's program. "Under the old regime," Philip Slowik, a grocery store owner in the village of Stanislowo, told me, "people struck when prices went up. Now the prices are rising but people don't protest because people trust the government. After all, it's the government we wanted."

"Now the prices are rising but people don't protest because people trust the government." —Philip and Aniela Slowik

This kind of optimism, at a time when many Poles are putting their cars up on blocks because they can't afford to register, insure or fuel them, reflects a kind of divine faith in the future of democracy and free enterprise. Naturally the impoverished people of Poland want a higher standard of living. But they are also ready to make enormous sacrifices to simply gain freedom of speech, thought and religion.

In the Soviet Union, 70 years of anti-religious indoctrination crippled many faiths. But in Poland, the home of the Pope, the church remains pervasive. One of the biggest challenges the Communists faced in Poland and other Eastern European countries

near Stanislowo, Poland

was selling atheism to a deeply religious populace. Father Edmund Jakacki, who heads the 23-village parish of St. John's, says the Communist anti-religious propaganda backfired:

"It had a boomerang effect. The more the government tried to discourage people from going to church the more people came. And why not? People were offended when the state tried to replace religious events like christenings by creating civil naming ceremonies for children.

"When the economy collapsed, many people lost faith in the government and went back to the church. They trust the church not because it will necessarily improve the economy but because it has been saying the same things for thousands of years. People trust the church more than the state."

Historic Cracow

2
Kicking the Tires

Morning mass finished, thousands of Cracow citizens on a sunny winter morning make their way across town to a muddy field that stands as their cathedral of capitalism: the Polish used car lot. Thousands of shoppers swarm over Polski Fiats and the inimitable paper body car, the East German Trabant. They kick tires on the Soviet Lada and crawl underneath the Czech Skoda to inspect for rust. Paying in cash, often inspected with a magnifying glass by the seller, these eager customers are at the heart of the great economic transition sweeping Eastern Europe.

The auto industry is one part of Warsaw's strategy to make the difficult transition to capitalism. In a nutshell, here's the government's plan in a country that now has about 4.5 million passenger cars: First slap a 70 percent duty on foreign imports. Then lay off part of the workforce at some of the nation's big car plants like FSO in Warsaw to make them more competitive in the export market. Next, sharply increase fuel taxes and car registration costs to raise revenue.

The immediate impact of this program has been to reduce traffic. But even Poles who can't afford to operate a car are eager to own them, an excellent investment at a time when the zloty's future is in doubt. Poles who have prospered by trading Eastern goods in the West or working abroad also have the money to buy these vehicles. Others are in a position to pay cash, thanks to generous relatives in the West. In many cases, relatives will pool their income

11

to buy a car they can share. Having money is one thing, but the used car lots give the Poles one of the most impressive and desirable advantages of capitalism: a choice. Like the rest of Eastern Europe, Poland has been without car showrooms since the Communists took over four decades ago. Under socialism, customers put down their orders for a new Polski Fiat at an office and then waited an average of five years for delivery.

But now, thanks to the Sunday car flea markets popping up in cities across the country, a cash and carry economy has arrived in the auto business. Poles can pick from a wide range of vehicles and drive their choice home on the spot.

Shopping in markets like the one in Cracow is complicated by the fact that there is no such thing as a test drive. Instead, the potential buyer and friends swarm over the vehicle in question looking for bugs, listening for rattles and using flashlights to spot fluid leaks.

Many of the vehicles in question have more checkered reputations than the Edsel. For example, the two-cylinder East German Trabant, a car that has traditionally taken 12 years for delivery in East Berlin, is reputed to be a vehicle that can get stuck on a piece of gum. Some drivers complain that horses like to chew away on the body, paper coated with fiberglass. The Soviet Lada car has heated rear windows, the saying goes, so that drivers can keep their hands warm when they push them on frigid days.

Be that as it may, plunking down bread for lemons is becoming a national passion. Yolanda, a young Cracow woman offering her 1973 Trabant for $550, was swamped with lookers in Cracow. "So what if the car is slow? It works and gets you where you need to go eventually." Yolanda, who wanted to move up to a late-model Czech Skoda, shares the widespread Polish bias toward foreign vehicles. Until 1990 Poles found it was quicker to go abroad to buy these vehicles. Some made big profits reselling foreign cars to their countrymen. But the new 70 percent car import duty has halted this trend and bolstered Poland's used car markets.

In Cracow, Jacek Kowalski, a grocery store owner, happily traded up on his Polski Fiat to a used Skoda for about $2,000. "It's a great deal of money," he admitted, "but at least now I'll have a car I can depend on." Adam, a construction worker, voiced similar

Used Car Lot, Cracow

enthusiasm for the East German Wartburg he had just picked up. "Why would I want to wait to buy a new Polish car when I get a reliable used vehicle like this one?"

Capitalist competition from the used car markets has prompted FSO, the nation's largest car manufacturer, to alter its marketing policies. For the first time, buyers of the firm's top-of-the-line Polonez can get on-the-spot delivery.

At the giant Warsaw car plant, executive Andre Fusnik told me: "The reason why delivery time has speeded up is that we increased the price from about $3,000 to $4,000," in a country where the average salary is $55 a month. "Only a limited number of customers have that much cash. Unfortunately there are still waits on the company's smaller, less-expensive models."

While some Poles like the idea that they can now buy new cars on demand, the Warsaw government believes the nation's auto industry must become more export oriented. At FSO, where annual production is 100,000 vehicles, down from 120,000 ten years ago, about half the cars go to the export market. "We do have some important advantages here in Poland," Fusnik says. "Our labor costs are a fraction of Western Europe's."

Deprived of traditional subsidies from government banks, many state industries must cut back to survive, but autos may be an exception. Deputy Labor Minister Jerzy Stretzer believes that Poland, a country that provided many of the skilled tradesmen who helped build the American auto industry, has excellent potential in the car market. Eastern Europe alone, where car sales have soared 59 percent over the past two decades to 42.7 million, is an excellent market.

Japanese firms such as Daihatsu are so impressed by the potential that they are discussing joint ventures with FSO, which makes Fiats under a license from the Italian firm. The deal is contingent on a Japanese government loan to the Polish automaker.

"Our problem," says Stretzer, "is managing the transition. One of the key issues for us is currency convertibility, making it possible to trade zlotys for dollars or marks. We are getting help from the International Monetary Fund and working hard to reduce inflation. Higher prices mean there are fewer shortages of basic commodities and more goods in the stores for people to buy. But with an end to government subsidies some factories will go bankrupt and at least 400,000 workers will be laid off this year."

Some other sectors of the Polish economy do have the potential to prosper in the new united Europe. The 1990 economic reforms, such as a tight cap on wages, higher consumer prices and phasing out inefficient businesses, were a prerequisite to the country's initial $1.725 billion credit package with the International Monetary Fund.

But it will take more than a line of credit to modernize the economy. Poles will have to work harder and lower their expectations in the short term to give Warsaw's grand plan a chance. Buoyed by the demise of Communism and the rise of their own Solidarity-led government, these industrious people believe they are perfectly positioned for a turnaround. But within this sea of opti-

Flower Stalls, Historic Cracow

mists, a few pessimists don't want to wait see how things turn out in the new capitalist Poland.

One of the happiest people at the Cracow used car market was Jerzy Starr who had just sold his used Polski Fiat for $1,000. "It's just too expensive to own a car here anymore. I'm moving to Australia."

Jiri Ruml—*Samizdat* crusader, editor of *Lidove Noviny*

3

The Patient Revolutionaries

Jiri Ruml has been called many things—subversive, liar, common criminal, seditious firebrand. But I prefer to think of the 65-year-old editor of Prague's hottest newspaper, *Lidove Noviny*, as a late bloomer.

Jiri Ruml is one of the faces behind the democratic revolution that has swept through Eastern Europe. While the story of the Communist empire's collapse is writ large, the energy behind this takeover comes from unknowns who used some of the smallest weapons in the political arsenal—the pen, the soapbox, the picket sign and the church pew. Across Eastern Europe, I met many people like Ruml, idealists who rejected invitations to join the Communist Party. Unlike millions of their countrymen who enlisted in the Communist machine simply to qualify for a good career or get their children into a good university, these people devoted their lives to the resistance. People like Ruml, Jewish leader Desider Galsky, Czech sociologist Ivan Gabal, and, in East Germany, Dr. Rudolph Weiner and seminarian Christopher Weber, may not win even a footnote in history. But they and thousands like them are the giants who brought democracy to Eastern Europe.

On the streets of Prague, in Berlin and Leipzig, East Germany, in Warsaw, Bucharest and Budapest it isn't hard to find people who played a part in the revolution. Our ambassador to Prague, Shirley Temple Black, told me that what kept this revolutionary spirit alive for more than four decades was an extraordinary patience.

17

"Between the end of World War I and the rise of Hitler, Czechoslovakia enjoyed a golden age of democracy and became the Switzerland of Eastern Europe," she told me on my first afternoon in Prague. "They had the patience and the resolve to recover what they had lost to the Communists."

"Before the November 17 revolution," Black said, "people would avoid eye contact. I'd take four- and five-hour walks and say 'good day' and they'd say nothing. Since then, people look up and excitedly talk to you." I signed Black's guest register right below communications czar Rupert Murdoch, who had been her luncheon guest. Downtown Naprikope Street was alive with talk that musician Frank Zappa had just flown in to meet the new regime.

Just as intriguing as the entrance of new faces is the exit of the old. As I walked along Naprikope Street, I spotted the Lenin Museum, now closed by the revolution. Eight husky workmen were removing a bronze frieze of Lenin's historic return to the Finland Station. I followed them inside where they placed it alongside other Communist flotsam, in a corridor outside the rest rooms.

Slipping in to a storeroom I found paintings and statues of the Russian revolution literally dumped into the ash can of history. And a few miles away, people from all over town were flocking in for their first look at the just liberated Praha Hotel. Located in a park-like setting, this Las Vegas–style establishment, complete with chandeliers, fountains and a health club, had been reserved for Communists and their guests. Here at rates around $30 a night, an incredible bargain, the party elite could enjoy the good life. There were even special stores in the hotel offering the party's closet capitalists luxury goods at a substantial discount.

"Like the special hospitals reserved for Communist officials," said Daniela Mankova, a student and information officer for Cedok, the national tourism office, who had come for her first look, "this was part of the party's double standard." Now being run by a new capitalist joint venture, the Praha was clearly benefiting from the revolution with room rates in the $150 range.

Exploring this fairytale city that was spared the ravages of World War II bombing raids, I discovered the faces behind this revolution belonged to people who never knew when to quit and even now are astonished by the swiftness of their own victory.

Visiting Prague today is a little like being part of a celebration of the Fourth of July, Thanksgiving and Christmas rolled into one. All over town from the Mala Strana district to Wenceslas Square, this liberated city was enjoying the fruits of victory. A playwright was running the country. Theaters were beginning to screen the once blacklisted films of Milos Forman and bookstores were unpacking the works of writers banned by the Communists such as Prague's Franz Kafka.

Emerging from 40 years of Communist domination, Czechs like Juri Ruml herald their newfound liberty every day. As a leader of the Czech journalistic underground this editor spent years in jail, endlessly harassed by the Communists and forced out of his chosen profession for 15 years. In a country where the truth could be found only on the sports page, his 500-circulation tabloid, secretly copied and redistributed across the land, was one of the few places in Czechoslovakia where you could learn what the Communists were trying to suppress. Today, now that press censorship has been lifted, circulation has soared to over 500,000 and the paper sells out within two hours of hitting the streets.

In Ruml's new office off Wenceslas Square the staff is still adjusting to its newfound freedom. The energy in these halls easily compensates for the lack of computer hardware and office auto-mation. After laboring so long in basements under the cover of night, secretly copying their underground journals, they now luxuriated in the comparative splendor of funky offices. "It's all so amazing," Ruml said as he poured a cup of tea. "I just finished taking a call from the president's office in the Castle. Havel would like to have a reporter accompany him on a trip to Warsaw tomorrow. Can you believe it? One day we're in jail and the next day we're on the presidential plane."

The editor of *Lidove Noviny* (*People's News*) was closely watched by the authorities ever since he began his career as a journalist in 1948. Founded in 1892, this independent paper was shut down by the Communist government in 1952 for unpatriotic reportage and went underground until 1988. Ruml's books, papers and articles in the *Samizdat* (underground press) were frequently cited on Voice of America and Radio Munich broadcasts. Unable to silence him by repeated jail sentences, the police, at various times during Ruml's career, seized six of his manual typewriters. Officially retired from journalism in 1960, the writer supported himself for 15 years driving a forklift before he resumed writing articles and books full time. All were panned by the Communists who sent him back to jail in 1981 and 1982 for subversion. "The fact that many leaders of the underground press, such as myself, went to jail and the *Samizdat* continued to appear kept the spirit of the revolution alive," he told me.

In 1989 Ruml was jailed again for another five years on charges of endangering society through his writing. In late November of that year, as one of his first official acts, President Havel freed Ruml and the rest of his nation's incarcerated journalists. "He also returned one of my typewriters that was confiscated by the Czech government," says the editor. Today *Lidove Noviny*, like the other free papers of Prague, has a rapt audience among patrons who are thrilled to finally have a chance to catch up on the true political history of the last 40 years. But in no way, insists the editor, is the paper an instrument of the new state. "Look here," he says, pointing to the first issue of the new above-ground edition. "On the front page we have a long letter criticizing Havel, the man who set me free. Under the old administration this kind of statement against the chief of state would have been a one-way ticket to the mental hospital."

Some of the staunchest opponents of the Communist regime, people like Desider Galsky, head of the Prague Jewish community, told me they had originally backed the Communists in 1948. "After the holocaust we thought they would be our best defense against the fascists," he told me. "Eighty percent of the Jews joined the Communist Party for this reason. You have to remember that in 1948 our Communist government was the only country in the world to send weapons to the Haganah to support their fight to create Israel. But then we learned about Russian anti-semitism. It was okay to be a Jewish doctor but not a hospital director. It was okay to be an editor, but not an editor-in-chief. What angered us and led to our participation in the opposition was the notion that Jews couldn't make it to the top even if they belonged to the party."

Galsky's office in the Jewish Town Hall was around the corner from the largest synagogue complex in Eastern Europe. Located in

Josefov, the old Prague Ghetto, these six temples served Prague's pre-World War II Jewish community of 50,000. Today they are part of Prague's State Jewish Museum, one of the finest collections of Jewish art and artifacts in the world.

Walking through these the sanctuaries I found beautiful textiles and silver works, Hebrew manuscripts, paintings and religious objects collected from the nation's synagogues during World War II by eminent Jewish curators. Selected by Hitler's lieutenants, these curators were told to create a "Museum of Jewish Culture" that would, after the inevitable Nazi victory, become a showcase of an "extinct culture." As Hitler's stormtroopers exterminated more than 90 percent of Czechoslovakia's roughly 100,000 Jews in the concentration camps, these experts were assigned to comb abandoned synagogues and ship the very best back to Prague.

In the capital city the temples became warehouses for this collection that would be exhibited after the Third Reich triumphed. "When their job was finished," said Galsky, "the curators were

Jewish Cemetery, Prague

rewarded for their hard work by being sent to the concentration camps. Some went to Terezin in the northern part of our country where they joined many other intellectuals, historians, singers and writers. That was the place where the orchestra rehearsed for a concert never knowing which members would be sent to Auschwitz."

After the war the Prague government decided to complete the State Jewish Museum, not as a memorial to a dead race, but as a tribute to Czech Jewry. Among the highlights are the Old New Synagogue, Europe's oldest synagogue, distinguished by its Torah shrine. In the High Synagogue I found one of Europe's finest exhibits of sacred Jewish textiles. Near this Gothic classic is the Baroque Cells Synagogue with an exceptional collection of Hebrew books and manuscripts.

The neo-Gothic Maisel Synagogue is famous for its handsome silver exhibit. In the Pinkas Synagogue were inscriptions memorializing more than 77,000 Czech Jews who perished in the holocaust. In the Jewish Cemetery centuries of graves, many built atop one another, have created hilly terrain. Adorned with poetic inscriptions, many of the tombstones list at sharp angles in this, one of the world's most beautiful graveyards. While the State Jewish Museum collection, which includes exhibits like children's paintings done in concentration camps, could hardly be characterized as an upbeat place, there is a happy ending of sorts to this painful story.

"The new government has restored complete religious freedom and people are beginning to return to synagogue," said Galsky. "We no longer have to ask the state for permission to have a festival or a special event. In the past we had to submit an official list of candidates for elections in our Prague Jewish community numbering about 1,000. Now we don't have to call anyone for permission to choose our leadership. The authority who used to handle this job under the Communist government is gone and I don't think he is going to be replaced. And there's something else I want to tell you. Today I feel we are more free than you are in America. In America it is very hard to succeed politically if you don't have a lot of money or know people who do. Today that's not necessary here. No one asks or even cares how much money Havel has in the bank."

A few blocks from the synagogue complex, I found a small crowd standing in front of a store window at the offices of Havel's

Charles Street Bridge, Prague

Civic Forum campaign office. They were watching videotape coverage of November demonstrations where police smashed young pro-democracy advocates. Inside, the office was doing a brisk business in pins and Havel posters put out for the spring elections. Sitting at the coffee bar, Ivan Gabal, a sociologist and Civic Forum official, explained another dissident strategy—silently agreeing with the Communist leadership while lending none of their expertise. "It was okay to publish and speak out abroad as long as I didn't publish here. By keeping the opposition alive in other countries we were slowly able to force the government into a corner. They claimed to have the people's loyalty. But from January, 1989 on they had to use riot police to control the citizenry. We were able to exploit their greatest weakness, the fact that the prime criterion for a position in the Communist government was loyalty to the party. They picked people who were unable to solve their problems.

"Under their system the most competent and creative people didn't enter politics. They were too slow and unprepared to deal with the political threat we posed. The fact that we remained non-violent, that we didn't smash windows, added to our power as the size of our demonstrations grew from 200,000 to 800,000 last fall. They didn't know how to handle civil disobedience."

Before heading off into a strategy meeting, Gabal mentioned one more cause that had attracted the attention of the Civic Forum. "We've been helping to raise money for victims of your California earthquake. People here are really worried about what happened to San Francisco."

4

Did Marx Drive an Edsel?

"Philosophers have interpreted the world in different ways. Now it's a problem to change the world." —Karl Marx

When I met Claus Freiberg, a Potsdam philosophy instructor and doctoral candidate, in the lobby of East Berlin's Humboldt University one rainy afternoon, a cup of coffee sounded like a good idea. But Freiberg knew better. "Nothing's open," he insisted, "this is not West Berlin." A minute later, my cup of coffee only a capitalist daydream, we were climbing a grand staircase past Marx's slogan writ large on the marble wall in six-inch-high steel letters. Why, I wanted to know, had Freiberg's party, the East German Communist Party, collapsed. Everywhere I'd been in Eastern Europe it was difficult to find anyone to defend Marx's faiths. Some flatly refused interviews. Others had turned in their party membership, and a few suggested that it was a miracle that the party had flourished as long as it did.

Even at one of the finest universities in Marx's Germany, professors were reluctant to explain this surprising revolution. Sitting down in an empty lecture hall as torrents of rain pelted the classroom windows, Freiberg proved more forthcoming. First he enumerated some of the good things the Communists had done for East Germany: "Rents were low, there were social service credits for families and parents as well as benefits for the elderly. Our nation

Hole in the wall, Berlin

was also much more anti-fascist than West Germany." So where had Communism gone wrong? As a philosopher, Freiberg brought an interesting perspective to bear.

"We have been taught that the only philosophy that's significant is the thinking that contributed to the development of Marxism," Freiberg suggested. "The party view is that Marx is the last philosopher we need to be concerned with. After studying Marx all we need to think about is reinterpreting Marx. Plato, Goethe, Voltaire—all the great philosophers weren't taught unless that had a direct connection with Marx's view." Marxist theory was classroom dogma for every student in the Soviet bloc. Equally important in the mind of Freiberg, who is completing his doctorate in comparative Greek and Chinese philosophy at Potsdam University, this view meant the virtual extinction of his profession. Last year, East

Germany, a nation of 16 million, enrolled exactly seven philosophy graduate students.

"Seven was the magic number," he told me. "One year they'd enroll seven in Berlin, another year seven in Leipzig, but never more than seven. You see, since philosophy ended with Marx, the party did not believe it was a very useful profession. Also, philosophers tend to be a very critical lot. This approach definitely hurt the country because people weren't encouraged to think freely. In the classroom, teachers didn't know enough to respond to questions creatively. Students never had a chance to study comparative philosophy and learn how other political philosophers thought. As a result they couldn't come up with creative ideas to help solve our many problems."

It was this gap between the theory of Marx, a 19th-century philosopher thinking about a revolution that was supposed to take place in an industrialized nation such as England or Germany, and the reality of 20th-century Communism, that led to the party's philosophical crisis. In theory Marxism was the ideology that would transfer control of society from the capitalist power elite to the working class. One true party of the people, the Communist Party, would chaperon the proletariat, making sure no one took advantage of the common man. For all the great theoreticians, Marx, Lenin, Engels and Trotsky, the central political issue was empowering the powerless who would then end centuries of oppression by the Hapsburgs in Eastern Europe, the czars in Russia and the bourgeois dominating the rest of Europe. These philosophers believed America's democratic revolution was suspect because it enfranchised an elite group of monopolists who made the rich richer while everyone else fought over leftovers.

Maybe the theory made some sense. But in practice that power never trickled down from the Communist leadership. It was Rita Klimova, Prague's new ambassador to Washington, who explained the breakdown clearly one morning at Hradcany Castle, the seat of Czech government. A former economics professor at Charles University, Mrs. Klimova likes to say she was "correctly purged" from the Communist Party in 1970 for supporting an historic uprising two years earlier. The ambassador is mindful of some of the important contributions the Communists made to Czechoslovakia since they were voted into power in 1948: "The Prague subway is clean and efficient. We have a pedestrian zone downtown. And there are pretty good child care and maternity benefits. That's the good news. The problem was that the Marxist medicine produced no cure and many devastating side effects."

Marx argued that after the Communists seized power there would be a transitional socialist period where the proletariat would become independent of the bourgeois. With the state guaranteeing economic security, the capitalists would no longer be able to play off the workers against one another. As competition declined, conspicuous consumption and wasteful overproduction would decline. Finally, and this was the key to Marx's dream, the state would no longer need to be a coercive instrument of the bourgeois. Since capitalists would no longer war with one another for economic advantage, peace would break out and the Army could be dismissed. The result would be a classless Communist society where the state would "wither away" into a mere caretaker.

"It didn't work out that way," says Mrs. Klimova. "The new leadership immediately tampered with all the important institutions of society, including the market economy, the church and charity. People began to get the idea that they didn't have to take care of themselves because the state was going to take responsibility for everyone. For example, Czechs began to think they could abuse their bodies by smoking and eating and drinking too much because ultimately the state health care system was there to take care of them." Far from withering away, the state became all-powerful by "tampering with the rule of law. The Communist Party had a monopoly on all the institutions of power, which meant anything its leaders wanted to do was legal. Let me explain.

"When Richard Nixon committed a crime in the Watergate scandal an independent judiciary and Congress was there to go after him. But when Ceausescu was committing genocide, selling babies out of orphanages and stashing the proceeds in his bank accounts, he broke no laws. After all, he controlled the legislature and the judiciary. That's the advantage a totalitarian enjoys, total control. Marcos had to steal to get rich. Ceausescu just helped himself. Under the Communist system he was not a crook."

The Brandenburg Gate, Berlin

In Prague I asked Gabriel Andrescu, a Romanian human rights activist from Bucharest, to explain why Ceausescu wanted to destroy the nation's 6,000 traditional villages, get people off the land and resettle them in Stalinist apartment complexes. "You have to understand," the young physics researcher said during a break at a human rights conference packed with recently liberated Eastern Europeans, "that when a man has his own cottage or farmhouse he is independent of the government. When you move them into an apartment house it's a lot easier to watch them."

Acting like a colonial power rather than the godfather of Communism that Marx would have wanted, the Soviets relentlessly tried to impose their culture on these states at the expense of national heroes and heroes-to-be. In the Czech schools every child was required to study 12 years of Russian. But in literature classes Prague's most famous writer, Franz Kafka, was not taught, perhaps because his classics such as *The Castle* were banned. Even a seemingly innocuous Prague band name like "The Tomahawks" raised the state's ire. That Indian term just happened to also be the name of an American cruise missile. The band was forced to change its name to "The Musical Group of Ondrej Heijma."

Just to make sure religion didn't make a comeback, many of the Communist satellites banned the Bible. I talked about this one evening with a Christian Scientist named Peter Landsinger. For more than 30 years this teacher, construction worker and salesman was forced to worship in the privacy of his own 250-year-old apartment. "Other denominations such as the Catholics and the Methodists were allowed to worship publicly," he said. "But the spiritual nature of the Christian Science church upset the officials."

Even those who committed no crime were still carefully watched in the police state. One afternoon I took a cab out to the apartment of Vladimir Duben, a 63-year-old draftsmen who dreams of one day visiting the United States. "No one escaped the watchful eye of the party," he told me. "My wife, a teacher, was required to file detailed reports on the students in her classes with a focus on any suspicious activities within their families. Even innocent people like me were closely scrutinized. Here, take a look." Duben's thick political file, just released by the Havel government, looked like what you might expect to find on a member of the underground.

"A lot of people were watching me for the Communists," he said as we looked over reports documenting his behavior, manners, food preferences, names of pen-pals in London, favorite television shows, books on his shelves, travels and the way he dressed. "I look pretty good on paper," he told me. "They didn't find anything wrong with me in nearly 40 years. It's an excellent dossier from my point of view. The Communists tried to be thorough but weren't very good at it. They never found out about the only crime I committed in my life, copying underground political newspapers aimed at overthrowing their government."

"Communism is Dead"—Prague

5

When to Say When

The nose was up and the landing gear down. Our flight was less than a minute from the airport and still there was no word from the cockpit.

Just before touchdown a stewardess ran up and down the aisle asking people to take their seats and buckle up. But even after we landed there was no information from the flight deck. Twenty minutes later our Russian-made Hungarian jet was still taxiing.

I began wondering if we had landed in Minsk and were driving to Leningrad. Finally, after half an hour, the pilot parked our plane, the only arrival that hour at the international terminal. An hour later our bags began to materialize and the Soviet passengers rushed toward customs.

Everywhere else in the world X-ray machines scan the luggage of outbound travelers. Here in Leningrad the process was a two-way street. A Russian man ahead of me, just back from a Greek holiday on the Ionian Sea, easily cleared X-ray and a lengthy inspection of his suitcase. But the security agent still wasn't satisfied. What exactly were these papers in his carry-on? The official searched diligently for *Samizdat* and other underground political literature, but all he came up with were glossy tourist brochures on the good life in Santorini.

Finally it was my turn. A luggage check revealed about what you'd expect on an American fresh from Vienna, Prague, Leipzig,

33

Berlin, Cracow and Warsaw: 10 pounds of the Berlin Wall, film of Czech workmen tearing down a bronze museum frieze of Lenin arriving at the Finland station, a loaf of fresh Polish pumpernickel, half a dozen English paperback dictionaries, three dozen valentines, twenty small boxes of candy "conversation hearts," a set of 45's including that kid's favorite, "On Top of Spaghetti and other songs to tickle your funny bone," and 20 cherry, blueberry, apple and chocolate chip granola bars. I was cleared in an instant.

Lenin, the Thomas Jefferson of the October Revolution, was right all along. Real revolutions weren't started by intellectuals sitting in 12-hour meetings but by factory workers and students, clerics and journalists, farmers and nurses, secretaries and store clerks, common people who never even rate a footnote but are simply fed up.

In the flood of analysis that comes with political transformation, process is often overlooked in favor of simple answers. Disillusioned party officials talk about corruption and try to characterize the fallen regimes as socialist banana republics. Others blame demented political forefathers like Stalin or Brezhnev. It also is tempting to suggest that the system collapsed because it never came close to responding to real human needs from the workplace to the hospital ward to the classroom.

But if you listen closely, there is another view that provides an important clue. In Leningrad, a student summed up some of her own disagreements with her father this way: "The difficulty is that he only thinks one way." Far too often that way turned out to be the hard way, the wrong way or both. Even when things were going right, they were often sabotaged by the system. A Soviet psychiatrist in Archangelsk, asked if a simple infusion of cash and equipment would improve the failing medical system, shook her head and said: "Of course not. They'd still screw it up."

You could blame this on self-destructiveness or sheer incompetence and perhaps be half right. At its zenith the Communist state is less a creation of Marx, Lenin and Engels than it is of their anonymous descendants, the bureaucrats who are ultimately loyal to process, not philosophy.

These are not simply the Gorbachevs, the Zhivkovs or the Honeckers, or, in some cases extravagantly paid political administrators. Rather, these are the bureaucrats who have created an empire so complex only they can understand, administer and enforce it.

The state, which was supposed to wither away under Communism, has become inescapable.

Nothing can happen until the bureaucracy lets it, which leads to a waiting game stretching into infinity. And it is frustration over this endless queue that led, at least in part, to the revolutions in Eastern Europe and to the rise of reformers like President of the Russian Republic, Boris Yeltsin, in the Soviet Union.

One common thread appears to unite Yeltsin and opposition groups now challenging the power behind the Soviet throne. After more than seven decades of rule in the grand daddy of Communist states, it is the bureaucrat who appears to be the greatest obstacle to meaningful reform. Replacing this vast red-tape army is Gorbachev's greatest challenge, a job roughly equivalent to George Bush replacing the Fortune 500.

Nevsky Prospekt ice cream queue

A historian in Vienna tried to explain the bureaucratic night-mare this way. "They have all the ice cream you want in the winter months, but not enough in the summer." She was half right. When I reached Leningrad there was plenty of ice cream available. The only catch was the hour long wait necessary to reach the vendor selling eskimo-type pies on Nevsky Prospekt.

To understand why the Soviet economic system is crippled, consider how a generation of paper pushers has stifled ambition, rewarded incompetence and humiliated a great people with a brilliant scientific, academic and artistic tradition. If as Engels suggested, religion is the opiate of the people, then surely the bureaucracy is the vodka of the Communist Party. Even the most dedicated Internal Revenue Service nit-picker would be astonished by the long arm of the Soviet bureaucracy. These career civil servants operating from a vast code, much of it unwritten, have created a waiting game that defies the imagination. They also have left an entire nation bewildered and confused. Try to imagine living in a country where used cars cost more than new ones, where badly needed medical equipment sits in warehouses uncrated or shopping in a store means waiting in three or four different lines to make a single purchase.

The old cars cost more than the new because people would rather shop the used market than wait five years for a new vehicle. The modern medical equipment withers away in the warehouses because no one has found the time or the manpower to get it installed. And those lines to get in a store, order a good, pay for it and finally return to pick it up have made the Soviets some of the most patient people in the world.

Consider 38-year-old Alex Harrucinov, an office worker. Several years ago, stuck in a low-paying desk job in a Georgian city, he decided to move to Moscow. For 4,000 rubles, about two years' pay, he bought a letter from a Moscow employer inviting him to join a firm in the capital. Officialdom was now ready to let Alex move to Moscow except for one small catch. He had to convince the city's housing bureau to assign him a room in a family flat. Consent could not be granted until the former occupant of the room got permission to move to another flat in the Ukraine. And of course that couldn't happen until an occupant of a Ukraine flat was given permission to move to Alex's old place way down south in Georgia.

"It took me 18 months for the three housing authorities to sign off on the paperwork." Difficult as Alex's story sounds, at least he finally got his flat and 150-ruble-a-month job in Moscow. But trying to join the perestroika revolution can be far more difficult.

Now consider the case of Mikhail Shahov, a Smolensk carpenter who joined a Soviet construction cooperative five years ago on the government promise that the workers would actually get to keep a share of their profits. To begin with, his firm is required to pay up to five times as much for raw materials as competitive Soviet firms run by the government/Communist Party. "And that's just one of our problems. If I tried to describe all the roadblocks the state bureaucracy puts in our way it would take two or three hours. You'd fall asleep before I was finished. But let me describe just one. Before we get one penny to pay our own workers the state confiscates 85 percent of our gross income through taxes and other measures. Of course we end up with nothing."

Shahov's example suggests precisely how the state bureaucracy protects itself against competition, thereby undermining the stated goals of the political leadership professing support for cooperative experiments. Even worse, the bureaucrats complicate life for no apparent reason.

Take, for example, a traveler who is required to surrender a passport to a hotel desk clerk. Instead of quickly noting your number on a registration form the clerk gives the passport to another clerk who keeps it overnight. This inefficiency is compounded when you arrive at another hotel for a business dinner and discover, to your horror, that another bureaucratic functionary won't let you in the door because you don't have a passport.

Now let's say that as a Soviet citizen in frustration you decide to get away for a few weeks. At the Aeroflot office in Leningrad the wait for a seat to New York, purchased in rubles, has stretched recently to 15 days. And after buying your ticket it is still possible to get bumped by a hard-currency customer.

Perhaps you'd like to phone your friend in New York about the delay. No problem, the operator is making reservations for international calls three days hence. Or, simply visit a hotel business center where your Fax will go through in 15 seconds. The only catch is no Fax phone lines are available until *zaftra*, that ubiquitous Russian word that means tomorrow.

The Russian minute, which seems at times to stretch toward infinity, is the unique creation of a generation of Soviet bureaucrats who have raised inefficiency to an art form. In the process they waste money, make it hard for people to get their work done and, in the words of one young man in Moscow "humiliate their country-men every day."

It's not surprising that the best cooking in the Soviet Union is done in private homes, beyond the reach of state-controlled restaurants where guests stand outside in the cold while idling waiters preside over half-empty dining rooms. Doubly frustrating to the Russian people is the fact that the bureaucrats have created their own system to get around the queues they have created for the masses. Rather than stand in line for medical care, food, housing, or consumer durables, the bureaucrats help themselves to all the necessities of life through separate stores, clinics and offices reserved for the elite. Obviously this cutting in line is infuriating to the rank and file.

Equally troubling is the fact that choice slots in college and the best jobs tend to go to the children of the same bureaucrats who have made the lives of their countrymen so deathly dull. Stripped of the political rhetoric coming out of the Kremlin it appears that the future of the Soviet Union belongs to those who can put the bureaucrats out to pasture and create a society that isn't always a line to be waited in or an obstacle to be overcome.

6

Doctor-nost

In early February 1990 people all over Leningrad were complaining about the weather. The icy Baltic blasts these Soviets took as their winter birthright were replaced by gentle breezes up into the 40s. The only way to do a figure eight was to visit an indoor skating rink, and cross-country skiing remained a distant dream. Without its winter mantle of ice and snow, the city looked like a church without a steeple.

Undeterred by this, the fourth mild winter in a row, Soviets hopefully donned their fur hats as they went out for a stroll on Nevsky Prospekt. At parties, global warming was a hot topic of conversation along with other themes dominating the media in this, the fifth year of perestroika. The thaw in the Cold War, the democratization of Eastern Europe, secession movements in the Baltic republics, ethnic skirmishes in Armenia and rumors that Gorbachev was on the verge of a major political reformation were all in the headlines.

There was also a human interest story hitting the front pages of Pravda and making national television newscasts every night. A 16-member California surgical team was saving the lives of young congenital heart patients beyond the reach of the Soviet medical system.

But on this sunny afternoon the American doctors were missing from their base, the operating room at Leningrad Children's Hospital

#1. While scores of parents from all over the Soviet Union waited in the pediatric clinic to learn if their children had been chosen for life-saving surgery, these doctors rode an Intourist bus across Peter the Great's city to the Kirov Military Medical Academy, a military hospital traditionally off limits to foreign visitors.

The team, led by Dr. Nilas Young from Oakland's Children's Hospital had been invited to watch some of the Soviet Union's top surgeons repair a heart defect. They saw that and the astonishing ability of Soviet doctors to improvise.

The assignment this day was to correct an atrial septal defect, literally a hole in the wall or septum that separates the small chambers of the heart's right and left sides. Unlike many of the city's antiquated civilian hospitals, this contemporary heart surgery facility was blessed with modern Western equipment such as a heart-lung machine, echocardiographs, pulse monitors, multichannel EKG's and cell-savers that help preserve blood and return it to the patient. This was Leningrad's heart facility of choice for civilians and military personnel sick and important enough to qualify for the best care available in the Soviet medical hierarchy.

In the Western world, repair of an atrial septal defect is an open-heart procedure where the heart is stopped and the patient kept alive by a pump called a heart-lung machine. While the mechanical device supplies blood and oxygen to the patient, the surgeons painstakingly repair the defect.

But Dr. Alexander Zorin, probably the best heart surgeon in Leningrad and certainly one of the finest in the Soviet Union, astonished his guests when he announced there would be no need for the heart-lung machine. He explained that Soviet surgeons, handicapped by a shortage of modern equipment and supplies, have come up with a creative solution: They can repair the atrial septal defect barehanded on a beating heart.

As the Americans looked on in amazement, he scrubbed down with a combination of formaldehyde (normally used as embalming fluid, not a sterilizing agent) and hydrogen peroxide. Then, instead of stopping the child's heart and putting him on the pump, Zorin made a small cut in the atrium, stuck his bare finger inside the heart and sized the hole. With his other hand he brought sutures in

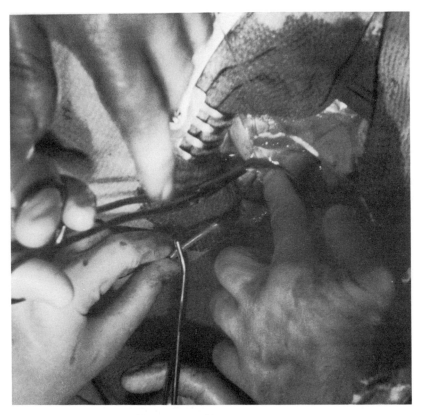

Bare-handed heart surgery

through the septum. Working entirely by feel, Zorin stitched around the hole and finally tied off the sutures to close the gap.

It was an astonishing feat, one that demonstrated the surgical artistry of the Leningrad doctors. For a variety of reasons, including the possibility of infection and the sheer difficulty of working on a defect you couldn't see, it was also an achievement the California doctors would never attempt to duplicate.

Now it was the Americans' turn to demonstrate one of their techniques, excision of an internal mammary artery for use in a coronary bypass procedure. Traditionally, surgeons grafted portions of a leg vein around diseased coronary arteries in this procedure. But recent American studies showed the internal mammary artery, which supplies blood to the rib cage, was more effective for the heart operation because, over time, it was less susceptible to subsequent blockage. Unfortunately this mammary artery is too short to complete the bypass operation, forcing surgeons to use it in combination with a leg vein.

As Dr. Young began his small part of the procedure, Dr. Zorin suggested that the American visitor take over the entire bypass operation. Unfortunately, hours before the Oakland doctors arrived, one of the Soviets accidentally disposed of the saphenous vein cut from the leg of the 40-year-old male patient for his heart bypass. Since it was inappropriate to retrieve the vein from the trash, Dr. Young asked his assistant, John Lee, to remove a second leg vein.

Lee called for a knife. But when he went to make the incision the instrument proved too dull to cut the skin. He called for a second, then a third knife without success. Finally Lee borrowed a technique he'd seen the Russians use. He pulled the skin taut, sawed back and forth and ultimately broke through to the vein.

As he sutured the patient, Lee remarked that the material seemed much stiffer than the silk and nylon fibers used at home.

"We're using linen," explained one of the Russian nurses.

"Linen?" asked Lee who had never heard of anyone using bedsheet-type fibers for surgery.

As Lee finished tying off the sutures and snipped away the excess, the Russian nurses didn't throw out their linen. Instead they squirreled it away for sterilization and reuse in a future operation, an unthinkable idea in the Western medical world.

After the new leg vein was prepared, Dr. Young, wearing his familiar checkered surgeon's cap, went to work. The California doctor was delighted by dome-mounted surplus tank lights providing the best operating room illumination he'd ever seen. And unlike some of the Soviet doctors working in a nearby operating theater, the Americans would not have to share their instruments with surgeons working on an adjacent case.

The open heart procedure began with Young pouring a warm sterile water solution over the man's heart. The case moved along swiftly until Young called for a knife to cut the clogged coronary

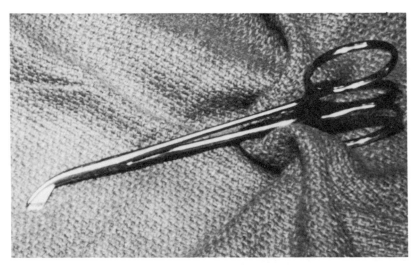

"The razor"—mounted in a surgical clamp

artery in preparation for the bypass graft. Again, a dull blade inter-
fered. Young called for a second knife then a third.

"We can't do this operation if we don't get something sharper.
We could lose the patient."

"Let's get the razor," suggested one of the Russian nurses.

"I thought it was a joke," Lee said afterward. "But a moment
later a scrub nurse handed Nilas Young a strange looking instrument. All of us stopped and stared. Here, in one of the best
operating rooms in the Soviet Union, they had just given us a corner
of a razor blade mounted in a surgical clamp. And it wasn't a very
sharp blade."

Fortunately this instrument, sterilized in the same formal-
dehyde/hydrogen peroxide solution used for more orthodox
instruments, was sharp enough for Young to complete the triple
bypass.

After completing the heart operation, Dr. Young asked a nurse
for another warm pitcher of sterile water to irrigate the pericardium
surrounding the heart. "We're all out," she apologized while re-
treating into another room. The surgical team waited in suspended

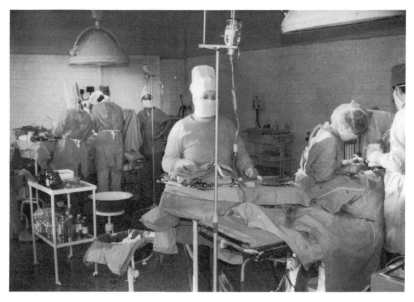

Two operations side by side at the military hospital. Surgeons working on the patients shared instruments from a common table.

animation as the nurse hurriedly poured a bottle of sterile water into a tea kettle and placed it on a hot plate.

Despite all these technological obstacles, the operation was an unqualified success, a testimonial to surgical improvisation and ingenuity.

"Given the limitations they are forced to live with," said Dr. Young afterward, "the Soviet surgeons do a remarkable job." Dr. Zorin was equally effusive. "Nilas Young," he declared, "is a great surgeon."

A few days later the Leningrad doctors were invited to a reception at the home of American consul general Richard Miles, the onetime residence of Aldra Mikhailovna, mistress of Grand Duke Konstanin Konstantinovich. "You're all we read about in the papers these days," Miles told Dr. Young as a national Soviet film crew taped an interview with the surgeon that would be aired the following evening.

The doctors and patients, high-ranking Communist party officials, Leningrad city leaders and the community's medical elite toasted the American/Russian program that was bringing new hope to thousands of congenital heart disease victims.

Over by the bar one of the consul officials pulled me aside just as I was about to help myself to more caviar offered by a liveried waiter. "Could you do us a small favor?" she asked. "A lot of American tourists, especially older people, don't understand the Soviet medical system. It's another world, so much gets lost in the translation and American patients can't handle it. We've got a situation now with an American woman in a Kiev hospital that you just wouldn't believe. When you get home would you please tell people coming to the Soviet Union to buy medical evacuation insurance?"

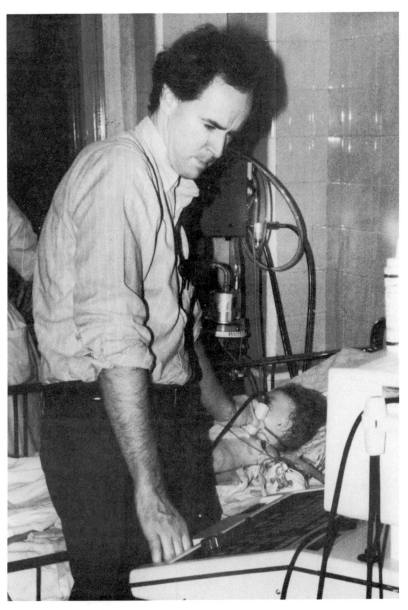

Cardiologist Gregg Helton examines a Soviet patient

7

Ten Young Lives Saved

It could have been a clinic anywhere in the Soviet Union. Children on the floor scribbled in coloring books while their fathers read them fairy tales. Mothers toting bottles and blankets—and cakes for the doctors—compared notes. Grandparents sat quietly, waiting for the family name to be called. But while this clinic had all the appearances of being rather ordinary, its mission on an overcast January day was rather special. By carefully watching the children you could see why they were there. They tired easily, some had a blue tinge to their lips, and several squatted periodically to improve their breathing.

More than 130 families had descended on Leningrad Children's Hospital #1 from distant cities like Smolensk, Minsk, Volgograd, Alma-Ata, Odessa, Kazan, Krasnoyarsk and Klaipeda as well as from the Leningrad region itself. One by one, they were ushered into an office with faded walls. There they talked through translators to doctors who could give the children the chance of living a normal life, something Soviet medicine could not yet offer.

The children were photographed with a Polaroid camera, examined by Oakland cardiologists Stan Higashino and Chris Hardy and then dispatched to a tiny room that looked like a school nurse's office. There another doctor, Gregg Helton, hooked them up to an echocardiograph machine that used sound waves to look at their damaged hearts.

Within a day their anxious parents were called back to see the Oakland physicians. A few got the best possible news: They could relax and go home, there was nothing seriously wrong with their children. Others received the worst news imaginable: Their critically ill children were inoperable. And 10 parents learned their children had been selected for life-saving heart surgery performed by the American team.

The medical plight of many of these children was similar to that of 7-year-old Maria Senotova, who in 1989 had become perhaps the most celebrated case in the history of Soviet pediatric cardiology. Now, a year after successful surgery, she hoisted her glass of Pepsi at the party assembled to greet the American team at her grandparents' flat on Leningrad's Maxim Gorky Street.

"I propose a toast," she declared with a maturity beyond her years, "to all the doctors who are saving the Soviet children."

Dr. William Feaster, the anesthesiologist from Oakland who knew Maria well, drank to that with gusto.

A year earlier, this little girl who was now gaily dancing around the room had arrived at Oakland's Children's Hospital an invalid. "Her heart disease was so severe," Feaster recalled, "that a lot of days she could barely get out of bed. She was starting to turn blue for lack of oxygen. Now look at her. She's got as much energy as any 7-year-old, maybe more."

The operation that saved Maria's life is a relatively common one in the United States and in many other countries. The basic procedure which improves blood flow to the heart and restricts excessive blood flow to the lungs is know as a "shunt and band." Performed all over the world in countries from the United States to China, it keeps children well until they are old enough for corrective open heart surgery. In our country 90 percent of the children born with this abnormality are saved. These children could have been easily treated in the West with off-the-shelf techniques. But each year in the Soviet Union, half of the 50,000 children born with congenital heart defects like Maria Senotova's die before their first birthday.

Until they found their way to Oakland, the Senotovas had been told their child's condition was inoperable. And like other grieving mothers, all that Elena Senotova was offered by her Soviet doctor was the consolation to "appreciate the fact that you're still young enough to have another child."

Maria's miracle might have been just that—a rare event other children in the Soviet Union could never dream of. But thanks to a year of hard work on the part of the Senotova family and friends, an Oakland foundation called Heart to Heart, physicians, nurses, translators, and hospitals in the U.S. and in the Soviet Union, more children like Maria are being treated and cured every day. During January and

Maria Senotova and Stan Higashino

February 1990, the 15-member Heart to Heart team from Oakland's Children's Hospital flew to Leningrad to perform pediatric heart surgeries. They also trained Soviet doctors to do similar operations.

"The surgeon gets a lot of credit," said Dr. Nilas Young, who operated on Maria at Children's Hospital in January 1989. "But believe me, you have to have an extraordinary team behind you to pull this off."

When parents of children with similar heart defects learned through the Soviet media of Maria's seemingly miraculous recovery, they deluged her parents, Elena and Boris, with letters. In a scene worthy of the great Russian novelists, the family would come home at night to find strangers on their Leningrad doorstep pleading for medical help. Moved by the outpouring, Elena Senotova contacted Jo Ann McGowan, an East Bay friend who had spent a year finding a surgeon and raising the money to bring Maria to Oakland for surgery.

The incredible frustrations of working out the diplomatic arrangements—a three-month wait just for Maria's visa that could have been granted by the Soviets in days—led McGowan to look for a new approach. At Oakland Children's, she, Dr. Young and cardiologist Stan Higashino began working on a plan to perform the surgeries in Leningrad.

Helping them was a neonatologist Victor Lvoff, a Soviet émigré whose own story adds even more flavor to the children's drama. His great grandfather, General Victor Kanshin, was hanged by the Bolsheviks in 1918. One of his grandfathers, Weinberg von Walhazen, was executed in Siberia in 1936 on espionage charges. His other grandfather, biochemist Lev Lvoff was executed in 1947 for advocacy of genetics at a time when this science was banned by Stalin. "Stalin subscribed to the pseudo-science of a man named Lysenko who contended that genetics was bourgeois. The whole notion of evolution was thrown out in the belief that the nature of mankind could be changed in one generation. Anyone who taught genetics, like my grandfather, was subject to immediate arrest," says Lvoff.

Five years after Lev Lvoff was executed, Victor's grandmother, Augustina Lvoff, died in a Soviet labor camp, a victim of a Jewish purge. So it was hardly surprising that on January 28, 1981, young Leningrad neonatology professor Victor Lvoff was summoned to the KGB office. Like his ancestors, Dr. Lvoff was accused of being an enemy of the people. He had foolishly published articles in an underground Samizdat publication, attacking the nation's neglect of pediatric care and soaring infant mortality rate. The fact that his article was correct proved irrelevant. "Overnight my passport was changed, forcing me to leave Leningrad, my home and my career," he says.

Hours before being sent off to exile in Siberia, Lvoff, through a family friend in the Leningrad police department, won a last-minute reprieve and fled with his wife, Eleanor, and their daughter to a refugee camp in Vienna. From there Lvoff and his family moved to Rome where Victor and Eleanor, a pediatric radiologist, made their living washing floors for a year. Many U.S. Embassy interviews later, they won political refugee status in America and moved to Boston where they supported themselves

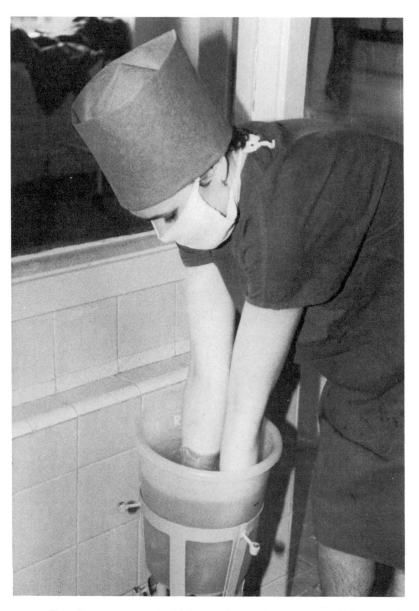

Russian nurse scrubs in formaldehyde/hydrogen peroxide

sanding floors for two years. Victor then interned at Boston's Children's Hospital, did his residency at Cornell and moved to the Bay Area where he completed three fellowships and received his Ph.D. in pulmonary physiology.

By the time Lvoff and the rest of the American medical team arrived in the Soviet Union in January 1990, the Heart to Heart group had raised more than $500,000 in donations. The Americans' arrival was national news in the Soviet Union. "People told us," McGowan said, "that so many times they'd been promised this kind of help from abroad and so many times nothing happened."

As the surgery team began to put hardware into place in the Soviet operating room, the American cardiologists began screening patients. Like many members of the team I had brought gifts for the children, little coloring books, records, bars of scented soap, small sponges that popped up into animal figures when they were immersed in water and Hershey Kisses. In addition to little gift bags, I gave each of the children valentine cards and candy conversation hearts that carried phrases like "kiss me" and "love you." Valentine's Day was an instant hit with the children in the clinic.

Working through a volunteer team of translators, many of them friends of the Senotova family, the doctors were able to deliver very good news to the parents of ten children scheduled for surgery. But the cardiologists had to deliver bad news to the parents of many other children. Sitting in their offices piled high with gifts of fruit and sweets brought them by the hopeful families, they had to look at young children who easily could have been saved as infants and explain that the heart disease was now inoperable. In the clinic outside, parents wept. Astonishingly, some of the children did not.

Photographer Virginia Clayton, who had traveled with the team, told a story about two patients who, in a gesture of friendship, had traded Polaroid pictures she had given each of them. When one 6-year-old girl asked for a second photo of herself, Clayton had to decline. She had only a limited supply of film and the doctors needed the photos for their patient charts, she apologetically told the blond child who had received one of my Valentine's Day gift packs the previous day. The girl persisted. "The doctor told me I'm

Nilas Young

one of the kids they can't help," she said. "I want to give my mother something to remember me by." Clayton, almost in tears, took the photo and handed it to the child. She almost squealed with glee.

It is easy to attribute the problems in Soviet medicine to budget limitations. But even discounting for the financial difficulties created by Kremlin bureaucrats, some anomalies defied explanation. The American doctors were concerned when they saw recovering surgery patients removed from respirators in the operating room and wheeled to intensive care before being hooked up to a ventilator supplying oxygen. The Heart to Heart team immediately remedied this dangerous procedure by hooking up a portable oxygen supply to each patient after surgery.

Five days after his arrival, Young, assisted by an American-Soviet operating team, performed his first successful surgery. Nine more cases followed, including a number of open-heart repairs. "The big surprise," the surgeon said over dinner one night at the canned-pea capital of Leningrad, the Pulkovskaya Hotel dining room, "was how smoothly it went. What was amazing to us was that they had never seen the most fundamental life-saving procedure in pediatric heart surgery—cardiac shunts and pulmonary banding designed to improve an infant's blood and oxygen flow.

"They know how to do more advanced procedures, but no one had ever taught them this technique, which is relatively easy to do and routinely saves children all over the world with congenital heart defects."

Just about everyone in the Soviet Union recognizes there is something wrong with the medical bureaucracy. In official publications, Moscow apologizes for the fact that "over the last 15 to 20 years the general level of health care in this country has not been what it should have." Many Soviet citizens complain that money that should be going to their medical system is diverted to the country's vast military and space programs.

In the operating room in Leningrad, American nurses Bea Morgan and Mary Ellen Connolly found their Soviet partners had devised innovative solutions to counter budget constraints. The husband of one of the Soviet nurses had designed and built an instrument table so functional the two American nurses decided to recommend it to their hospital in Oakland.

A godsend for the 10 children, the American team was of huge benefit to Soviet medicine as well by teaching doctors there the techniques of this life-saving surgery. When it was his turn to operate, Soviet surgeon Nikoly Kislev began swiftly, slowing down the procedure only at the suggestion of his assistant, Dr. Young. By the time he had finished saving the life of a little Soviet girl, it was clear that pediatric heart surgery would never be the same in Leningrad.

8

Deadly Health Care

One of the first questions the American doctors asked when they arrived in the Soviet Union was how a country that pioneered preventive medicine and natural childbirth, cut its infant mortality in half between 1913 and 1930, and does sophisticated heart transplants could fall so far behind the West in health care.

As it turned out, that question touched a raw nerve that is felt throughout the Soviet Union. No subject—be it breakaway republics, a floundering economy or the folly of Afghanistan— proved a greater source of national dismay than the Soviet health care system. I heard non-ending horror stories about botched operations, inadequate treatment and endless waits for treatment. At one point a hotel operator, unable to reach any of the doctors I was traveling with, turned in desperation to me for advice on how to care for her asthmatic mother. Russian physicians, whose industry and devotion were impressive, confessed that they did not even recommend the food served in their own hospitals. "I felt so sorry for the children in the hospital," an Archangelsk doctor mentioned one morning, "that I brought my own food for them from home."

So why is a country capable of producing sophisticated, horribly destructive weaponry simply incapable of producing edible meat and potatoes for its hospital patients? Before leaving for the Soviet Union I listened to Dr. Yelena Bonner, the widow of physicist and human rights activist Andrei Sakharov, attribute part of the problem to a lack of basic public health standards. In addition, she cited epidemics that can be traced to the fact that one-quarter of the nation is unfit for human habitation due to excessive air and water pollution, radioactive contamination and overcrowding.

Today, 20 million families have less than 7 square meters of living space per person, a figure the government calls the official minimum. Pollution has caused so much liver disease in the Aral Sea region that the army has difficulty getting its quota of draftees out of Central Asia. Out of the 30 developed countries, the Soviet Union has the lowest longevity rate. Infant mortality, after declining for 50 years, has been rising since 1976 until today the country ranks 53rd worldwide.

The ability of the Soviet medical system to address these problems is seriously hampered by facilities that seem to have more in common with the Middle Ages than the 20th century. For 80 percent of the rural Soviet hospitals have no running water or sewer hookups, breeding epidemics in regions where more than 120 million Soviet citizens live, about 40 percent of the country's population. There also are serious sanitation problems in the metropolitan areas. During a European television interview with Soviet doctors at a Moscow children's hospital not long ago, a rat scurried across a ward.

As the Soviet medical system has deteriorated, the public has become painfully aware of the cost of failing to keep up with Western medical standards. Soviet-produced medical equipment is in short supply and poorly made at that, and the government, plagued with a nonconvertible currency, can't provide the funds necessary to pay for necessary goods abroad. The quality of antibiotics is so questionable that doctors are sometimes reluctant to use them to treat pneumonia. The lack of disposables and inadequate sterilization procedures has led to iatrogenic outbreaks of infectious hepatitis.

Nowhere is this problem more apparent than in pediatric medicine. Dr. Nikolai Shabaloff, the Soviet Union's top neonatologist, told me, "You know, Soviet medicine was supposed to be built around a Lenin saying: 'The best to the children.' But that never happened. Instead, the money went to the military and the space program. Whatever was left went to medical care."

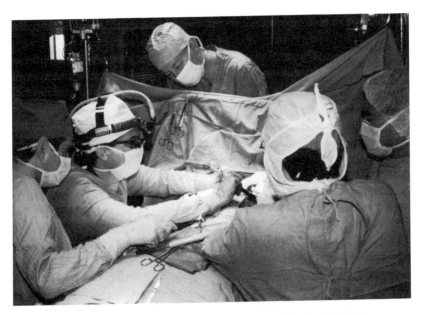

Nilas Young (with headgear), Alexander Zorin (center),
John Lee (right)

In specialties like pediatric cardiology the lack of equipment
and training has led to some unorthodox therapies. In most
countries perinatal asphyxia, an oxygen deficiency, is treated by
putting children on a ventilator that assists their breathing. But due
in part to a shortage of ventilators, a pseudo-science has evolved
here that prescribes megadoses of vitamin B_1 on the theory that
they would help the tissue absorb more oxygen. Unfortunately this
approach doesn't work.

Making matters even more aggravating, proper care is available—if you're cut from the right cloth. While the Soviets boast that
their socialist health care system is free to all comers, there is a
definite pecking order both in quality and price. Special hospitals
ranging from elite Kremlin clinics to medical facilities cater to
Communist party apparatchiks, professors, and other elite groups,
with care that is simply out of reach of the masses. It is here that
some of the best equipment, Western medicines and prompt atten-

tion is available. Dr. Gregory Khozin, a professor at Moscow State University, told me that the hierarchy imposed at these clinics is hardly consistent with the notion of a classless society.

"When I go for treatment, the clerk at the door asks if I'm an assistant professor or a full professor. The assistant professors go to the clinic on the fourth floor, and the full professors go to the seventh."

While Gorbachev has announced his intention to break up the special clinics and begin redistributing some of their modern equipment to clinics at large, the Soviet health care system remains blighted by a system of cash payoffs that were not the sort of thing Marx had in mind. Vastly underpaid doctors and nurses are often forced to moonlight by taking private paying patients or, in some cases, even resorting to prostitution to make ends meet. Other specialists, even relatively well-paid ones, require cash payments before they will even look at a patient. One morning on the way to the clinic at Children's Hospital #1 in Leningrad, Dr. Victor Lvoff, the Soviet émigré who was one of the Oakland physicians making the trip, told me about one of his Leningrad professors in the early '70s, the late Alexander Tur. No subway strap-hanger, Tur, perhaps the most famous pediatrician in the Soviet Union, owned white and black limos. The students speculated that using the white limo meant he was in a good mood, the black a bad one.

"Tur had also been a professor of a student who was to become my mother-in-law. One day when her daughter, my wife-to-be, took ill, Tur was asked to treat her. The professor insisted on 75 rubles to see her, just like any other patient. When her mother pointed out that she only earned 60 rubles a month, Tur was unyielding: 'No exceptions.'"

Lvoff went on: "Treatment at any specialty hospital required special payments. You might have to tip the administrator, the surgeon, and even give the nurse a ruble to change the bed. When I was teaching medical school, another professor's husband came down with rectal cancer. She tried to send him to a special Leningrad oncology hospital that charged 8,000 rubles. When my friend said she only had enough to pay 4,000 rubles down and 4,000 rubles after the operation, the surgeon refused to extend professional

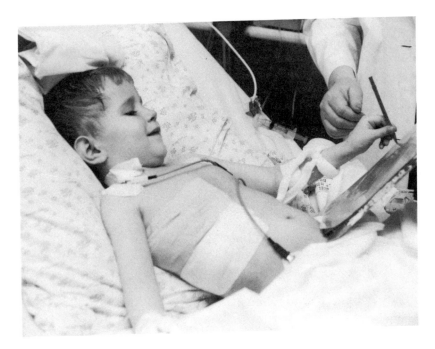

Sasha Kotov

courtesy. 'No exceptions for colleagues,' he said as he postponed the surgery date until she showed up with 8,000 rubles."

In much the same way that free medicine has become a cash-and-carry system, there also are great contradictions between adult and pediatric care. With adults, physicians tend to put on rose-colored glasses. At Leningrad Children's Hospital #1, I met a pathologist who explained that doctors were reluctant to give an adult patient bad news about incurable diseases. "For example when my husband came down with cancer they told me the truth. But they told him it was a blood disease." This euphemistic bedside manner is rationalized on the theory that a positive outlook can help the patient live a longer and healthier life. But many of the Soviet parents I talked to told me this was not the case in pediatric medicine. For example, Elena Senotova, whose daughter was treated in the celebrated Oakland heart case, was told time and again that there was no chance her ailing girl could be saved.

Even health care professionals have trouble getting accurate information. Natasha Shahov, a nurse from Smolensk, had wearied of carting her ailing 3-year-old-son, Misha, to specialists who basically shrugged their shoulders. In frustration, she went to the medical library to learn about her son's congenital heart abnormality. There she discovered that there was only a 1-in-100 chance that her boy would live to the age of 10, something the specialists had never told her. Then in January 1989, she picked up a newspaper and learned that Maria Senotova, whose ailment was similar to Misha's, had been successfully treated by Oakland surgeons—something else she was never told of by the Soviet doctors. "Just knowing the truth, that there were hospitals outside the Soviet Union where Misha could be saved, gave us hope," said Shahov. That very day, Natasha and her husband, Mikhail, began writing to everyone they could think of who might help them get their son to an operating room in Oakland. As it turned out, the Shahovs and nine other Soviet families didn't need to travel to California. The American surgeons came to see them in Leningrad in January 1990.

When I met him in the philodendron-shaded waiting area during his son's operation, Mikhail Shahov told me: "Until the Americans arrived it was like living on top of a volcano." For the Shahovs it was a miracle to be in a pediatric hospital where they didn't have to listen to apologies or watch doctors shake their heads. The words "nothing can be done" and "sorry" had been replaced by a nurse emerging from surgery to report: "The operation was a success. Your son will be able to lead a normal life."

A number of Soviet physicians were intrigued as well by the arrival of the American doctors. A few took it upon themselves to phone parents and urge them to take their children to the Leningrad special clinic—set up in June 1989 by visiting American doctors—where the January 1990 contingent would stop. Among those who received a call were Ludmila and Anatoly Kotov of Pedrodvorets. Eager to be first in line, the Kotovs made sure their son, Sasha, was in the Leningrad hospital well before the American doctors arrived. As a result, he was one of the first selected for the January surgery. Like many of the patients, Sasha had developed slowly and was unable to walk until he was 2½. Five days after the operation he was darting about his room, immersing in the sink some of the sponge animals I had brought.

"When he was 3 years old the doctors told us he would not be able to lead a normal life," Sasha's mother said. "Now, he wants to be a journalist."

Sophia Godina, mother of 14-month-old Jenia, a child operated on for a rare abnormality, was similarly overwhelmed. Like many of the other parents, she became active in a group formed to assist the visiting doctors with necessities like taxis and food. They saw the arrival of the Americans as a once-in-a-lifetime opportunity. Many of them described the treatment as a mystical experience and suggested that their children had been saved by God.

For people accustomed to cash payment to surgeons, specialists and hospital staff, the generosity of the American doctors was astonishing. Many asked Lvoff how much the Oakland doctors were being paid for their time and modern equipment. He recalled: "At one consulate party, a Soviet official pulled me aside and whispered, 'Come on, really, what kind of money are you getting for this?' When I told them the truth, that everything had been donated, they suggested I was either lying or crazy, maybe both."

Monument to the Heroic Defenders of Leningrad, World War II

9

This Is The Twilight Zone

Shortly after returning from Eastern Europe and the Soviet Union I was asked to speak about their political convulsions shaking the world. Sharing the podium with several Soviet families on a year-long exchange visit, I found that they, like many other Russians in our country are deeply homesick. But after I spoke of such problems as inferior medical technology, lack of a convertible currency, nuclear pollution, high infant mortality and a shortage of consumer goods, one speaker begged to differ. "The problem with you," she said, "is that you are much too optimistic."

After the laughter died down, someone in the audience asked if she could contrast the difference between the lifestyles of Soviet and American women. "In some ways they are the same, in others they differ," she said. "In both countries the women do all the housework. But in the Soviet Union they have less to clean."

This sense of black humor speaks volumes about the magnitude of the economic crisis facing this part of the world. Not only are their planners up against an entrenched bureaucracy that has systematically undermined almost any economic progress, but they also confront a populace that just doesn't believe in them. To this you can add economic stagnation that puts Eastern Europe and the Soviet Union on another planet compared to Japan and the United States. And then you can throw in the attitudes of people like Alex Harruczinov.

On the day of Gorbachev's decision to relinquish the Communist Party's political monopoly, I sat in a Moscow taxi trying to explain the concept of bankruptcy to my friend Alex. We were on our way to see two of the Soviet Union's most eminent economists, and Alex, my translator, clearly had a thing or two to learn about capitalism.

"I hear what you're saying," he told me, "but I don't understand. You mean that if someone can't pay his bills it's possible that the people he owes will come and take away his car or his house?"

"Yes," I said as we swung into the driveway of the Moscow Financial Institute.

"That could never happen here. The people wouldn't stand for it."

You can call that naivete or just plain ignorance but for Soviet and Eastern European planners, it's called reality. As these nations move to a Western economic system, their people are about to learn its flip side: that capitalism provides a lot of toys to consumers but also can be pretty heartless when they don't have the bread.

As Vyacheslav Shenayea, dean of the Moscow Financial Institute's international economic relations faculty, told me: "It is hard to instantly stop a loaded train. There has been much talk about perestroika, about economic reform in the Soviet Union. But the old principles are still in our brains." Cynicism about success. Dark Age economics. Naivete about what is to come. With such daunting obstacles, where do economic planners even start?

Gorbachev's plan is to sell government factories, let low, state-controlled retail prices increase, free most wholesale prices from state control, introduce a stock market and Western-style banking, and provide for private ownership of business. Together this represents the biggest economic change since Lenin's New Economic Policy. But experts like Shenayea believe real progress hinges on the convertibility of the ruble to foreign currency. From Wall Street to Frankfurt to Tokyo, the international financial community is listening to Soviet proposals to turn the devalued ruble, which officially trades at 1.8 rubles to the dollar (tourists get a special rate of 6 rubles to the dollar), into a currency that can be freely traded for Western goods.

Like Third World nations, the Soviet Union finds itself unable to buy the modern technology it needs to upgrade factories, increase production of consumer goods, modernize medical care and clean up its environment. This is partly because it lacks convertible currency and sufficient foreign exchange like dollars or marks. Another reason it can't buy this technology is that Moscow simply doesn't have the money, whatever the currency. Saddled with decades of over-spending on defense, the Soviet Union ran up a 1989 deficit of 92 billion rubles or 10 percent of its gross national product. In addition to heavy military spending, the economy is afflicted with low taxes by underpaid Soviet workers, low productivity that forces the country to import everything from wheat to medical equipment, an inability to attract foreign capital necessary to modernize industry and low quality of Soviet goods making them unattractive on the world market. Not every company is willing to engage in barter like Pepsico Inc., which trades its cola for Soviet freighters as well as the exclusive right to market a popular Russian vodka in the United States.

Only through foreign investment and improved productivity do the Soviets stand a chance of salvaging their ailing economy. "And that is very difficult to do," Dr. Shenayea told me, "when Western nations will not accept our ruble in payment." In 1989, devaluation of the ruble was the first step toward setting a realistic value for the Soviet currency. Creation of a guaranteed foreign exchange rate for the ruble would let Soviet or foreign enterprises lock in the value of a transaction for up to 12 months against the average value of a group of Western currencies such as the dollar, mark, yen, pound and Swiss franc. Now Soviet officials are entertaining many other possibilities such as using some of the nation's vast stockpile of 6,200 tons of gold, the world's largest, to back up the ruble on world markets. Another idea is to soak up some of the 600 million rubles held in low-interest savings accounts by selling bond certificates that Soviet citizens could convert into Western currencies. This would give them the hard currency necessary to buy dearly needed foreign goods or travel abroad. The Soviets also are interested in requiring former socialist trading partners such as Poland to begin paying off their debts.

But the problem with all the suggestions is the same one that got the Communists in this fix in the first place—the system just creaks along when what it really needs is a pace car.

Consider the chemical industry, which even Soviet Prime Minister Nikolai Ryzhkov concedes can't compete in the world economy. Its factories are antiquated, its bureaucratic bosses tied up in knots and any suggestion of industrial progress runs up against a concern we in the West are familiar with: the environment.

While the bureaucrats believe industrial progress is a cornerstone of perestroika, the Soviet people have indicated in survey after survey that cleaning up the environment is their number-one priority. State industries and the Kremlin insist they are not ignoring the Green Movement, the largest coalition of new political groups in the Soviet Union, but Leningrad chemist Valentin Yemelin insisted: "Gorbachev is trying to save factories that don't have the money to upgrade. The problem is that we are talking about life or death issues. The Chernobyl disaster was one obvious example with consequences far beyond our borders. You also know about the Aral Sea nightmare, where diversion of water to supply cotton fields, a principal source of Soviet foreign exchange, has dried up much of this vast inland sea. This in turn has led to dust storms that have coated the region with harmful pesticides. As a result, northwest Uzbekistan now has the Soviet Union's highest infant mortality rate.

"But what you haven't heard about is an Armenian chemical plant in Yerevan that makes resins used for synthetic rubber used in tires and other products. This is a basic Soviet industry, a crucial plant. They had to close it because it was stinking up the whole city with a chlorine leak, a very dangerous problem. But now a shortage of resin is hampering Soviet industry and leading to pressure to reopen the factory at the risk of people's health."

The environmental nightmare extends across the Soviet Union and its one-time Eastern Bloc. Public health experts estimate that in terms of illness, reduced productivity, disability benefits and environmental damage, the Soviet bill for pollution runs 240 billion rubles, roughly 26 percent of the Soviet gross national product. Harmful nitrates dumped by Czech industry has forced that country

The Wall Fire Sale, Berlin

to ban drinking water for infants. In industrial areas, where life expectancy is 15 years below the national average, Czechs joke that the Communist government was the only one that practiced chemical warfare against its own people.

In East Germany most cities have air pollution 50 times the maximum considered safe, 80 percent of the rivers are contaminated and more than a third of the trees are dead or damaged. Its factories spew more sulphur dioxide contamination than any other nation in the world. In Cracow, one of Poland's most important tourist centers, more than 700 stacks at the infamous Nowa Huta steel mill belch toxic fumes into the air each day. Compounding the problem is that Western European nations, decrying this pollution as a source of acid rain and water contamination, freely use Eastern Europe as a dumping ground. For example, West Germany has exported toxic wastes to East Germany for decades.

Students of the crisis told me they doubt people will succumb to industrial pressure that has gutted attempts to protect the environment in the past. In the spring of 1990 Soviet environmentalists challenged an Occidental Petroleum plan to build a chemical plant in the Ukrainian town of Kalush. Their sharp questioning of the plant's environmental impact persuaded the American company to put the joint venture on hold.

Then again, there are situations like the Isthmus of Karelia, bounded on the west by the Gulf of Finland and on the east by vast Lake Ladoga. A favorite vacation spot for Leningrad residents, it offers beautiful cruising through the Vuoksa Passage, a chain of small lakes and streams that link the Gulf with Ladoga. Carpeted with lovely pine forests, the perfect place to forage for berries and mushrooms or fish for trout and salmon, this region is also an important Soviet wildlife refuge. Unfortunately, Soviet industry appears to be threatening to turn the Isthmus of Karelia into a Russian Love Canal. Untreated pulp plant effluent, oil pollution, and lake-destroying gravel production all contaminate the area. In the village of Kamenogorsk, West German equipment has already been delivered for a factory that will produce formic acid. This, in spite of the government prohibition against constructing new industrial enterprises in the Lake Ladoga watershed, which now barely copes with the pollutants it receives.

At his Lenin Hills apartment Moscow State University Professor Gregory Khozin told me of some of the environmentalists' obstacles. Noting the huge costs of equipping obsolete plants with pollution-control devices, he said that simply retrofitting scrubbers on existing power plants to cut sulphur dioxide pollution will likely hike the cost of products as much as 50 percent. What we need to do is design pollution controls into every new factory we are creating. Until our government accepts modern health standards and includes the price of these improvements in the cost of doing business, we will not be able to truly clean up our environment. It's hard for us to get started when we are only beginning to create the pollution monitoring network we need."

It's quite possible that the West will pay at least part of the cost of these improvements. Already, West Germany has agreed to contribute more than $500 million to help clean up East Europe's obsolete industries, including many built during the Third Reich. In the process, modern plants will be built to help create new jobs for some of the 10,000 East German workers let go when their polluting factories are shut down. Scandinavians, aware that it costs 20 times less to get rid of a ton of sulphur dioxide by paying for scrubbers on a foul Polish factory than adding high-tech devices to their own, squeaky clean stacks, are considering helping out their Eastern European neighbors. And the Bush administration has invested $20 million for pollution control in Poland and Hungary.

The Soviet Union, which lacks the technology to clean up its chemical plants or the funds to buy necessary pollution control equipment from the West, is another candidate for this kind of aid. Hard currency is, of course, necessary to buy modern scrubbers. But Prime Minister Ryzhkov points out that if the Soviet chemical industry began selling its products at world prices, red ink would quickly sink these plants. This is why pollution control grants from the West are an important first step toward putting Soviet and Eastern European industry on an equal footing with the West.

Can these programs clean up the environment of this region and help their industries become competitive on a world scale? "They have to," said Leningrad environmentalist Yemelin. "This is one issue that the people have already decided for the government. If they don't make substantial progress on cleaning up industry, the people will simply elect a new government." But as the overhaul begins, it is obvious to many leaders of these countries that they are a long way from the level playing field they dream of. "Until we achieve convertibility and bring in the kinds of joint ventures we need to modernize our economy, real economic progress is going to be very difficult," said Shenayea.

Olga Mordinova, a 10th-grader I spoke with at Moscow Public School #45, told me she believed the Communist government will probably rise or fall on modernization of the economy. "People are eager to change, to experiment. For example, I'm interested in studying foreign trade as a way to help solve our economic problems. If the Communists can't do something about our economic situation, if they can't improve life, they are going to have a harder time competing against the new parties. Their political crisis may make it impossible for them to solve our economic problems."

Perhaps this is why Soviet officials are now considering the ultimate solution to the economic crisis. They are weighing a proposal to offer a $25,000 prize to the Soviet citizen who devises the best plan for making the ruble convertible into hard currency. The prize, of course, will be paid in hard currency.

10
Yuri's of Leningrad

Like everyone who travels abroad, I'm no stranger to the black market. From Shanghai's Bund to the back streets of Dubrovnik, black market operators can be heard whispering sweet nothings like "Change money?" in your ear. And in Prague, nearly everyone is familiar with a dark movie drama called *Bony A Klid* (*Bony and Quiet*), in which a teenager is lured into the black market. The film portrays the friendly "Let's Make A Deal" chaps on the street as mere foot soldiers in criminal syndicates ruled by capitalist princes. Not only did I encounter my share of black marketeers on my trip to Eastern Europe and the Soviet Union, but I also found that they too are not immune to hard times. Because of currency devaluation in Poland, Czechoslovakia and the Soviet Union, black marketeers have been in a slump. "For us," a black market quick-change artist told me in Prague, "the official exchange rate is about what we can pay." In Warsaw, another sidewalk money man told me: "At this point the best reason to change your money on the street with us is that our lines are a lot shorter than the banks'."

Enter Yuri of Leningrad, one step ahead of the law and light years ahead of perestroika, as an operator in what is sometimes called the only functioning part of the Soviet economy. "If you don't mind," Yuri told me after we met outside the Russian Museum, "I'd like to talk to you away from all the police hovering around this place." A few minutes later we were at a café where 21-year-old

71

Yuri and his 16-year-old friend Maxim were treating me to tea and ice cream.

Yuri, who has been in the black market since 1984, told me he grosses about 200 to 300 rubles daily in a country where salaries run roughly 150 to 400 rubles a month (about $25 to $67 at the official tourist exchange rate of six rubles to one dollar). In the summer a good day can run as high as 600 rubles. The heart of his business, changing money, is centered around selling the dollars he buys at 10 to one to other Russians for 14 to one. While he does not have many of the problems that plague Soviet industries seeking foreign investment such as a shortage of raw materials, outmoded production methods and products that can compete in Western markets, Yuri finds it's not easy to attract capital from abroad.

When I talked to him a few months after the Soviet Union lost its grip on Eastern Europe, he told me that soliciting business on the street was frustrating. "I might talk to 100 foreigners a day to find one customer who wants to change money. Even though I offer 10 rubles for a dollar (much better than the official tourist exchange rate), many people aren't interested. Many tourists know it's easier to shop with dollars than rubles. A lot of people don't want Russian money, except perhaps as a souvenir."

A student of international finance, Yuri told me he is eager to see the ruble become a currency that can be freely traded for Western goods.

"Like everyone else in this country we need dollars. Let me explain it this way. If I had a lot of dollars I would go to Helsinki and buy the same kind of running shoes you have on. They are very valuable here, worth even more than blue jeans. But the only way I can get them is with hard currency. With rubles all I can get are Russian shoes and no one wants them. By the way, I'd be willing to give you $30 right now for those Nikes you have on." I declined.

A former student at a Leningrad economics institute, Yuri dropped out after he decided there was no future in the conventional business world. "My wife is seven months pregnant. I want to get a better flat. It would be impossible for me to do that with the kind of pay my professors made at the economic institute. The car I own would take at least 10 years to pay for on a normal Soviet salary."

As an entrepreneur, Yuri told me he is keenly interested in some of the Soviet government's radical economic reforms such as letting low, state-controlled retail prices soar to free-market levels, introducing a stock market, launching Western-style banking, the leasing of real estate and, especially, worker or private ownership of many businesses. The problem, he explained, is that many Soviets, particularly those in state-owned businesses, feel threatened by a new generation of cooperatives and entrepreneurs:

"Take the quality of what I'm selling. You've seen my fine watches. In a government store you may not even be able to find this product and certainly not at such a good price. This jacket I have on comes from Finland. It's much better looking than what you can find in a Soviet shop. Right now only foreign tourists and a few Russians can afford to buy it. But what happens when someone

Mr. Yuri's Neighborhood

like me starts importing this kind of product and sells it next door to a state-owned clothing store? Obviously we're going to be taking away a lot of their business. The thought of real competition scares them.

"The fact that we are successful creates a lot of problems. In Russia we have these guys called boxers, I think you would call them gangsters, who beat you up if you don't pay them off. One slugged me three days ago. Fortunately the police are easier to deal with. I give the local sergeant 100 or 200 rubles a week and the same for his boss."

As we talked and finished our ice cream, Yuri's friend Maxim placed a tin of caviar in front of me, hoping I would make an impulse buy. He explained that most of the watches, KGB T-shirts, military uniforms and other goods sold on the black market come from kingpins who control broad territories. "We also shop sales abroad," said Yuri. "For example take a jacket that costs 400 rubles in Finland. After Christmas we can buy it in Helsinki for 75 percent off and then sell it back here for a big profit. Our best foreign customers tend to come from America, West Germany, France, Sweden, Finland and Denmark. Tourists from the socialist countries are terrible. We try to avoid the Poles and the Yugoslavs."

Maxim, who gives 200 rubles a month to his widowed mother, says he enjoys the perks of the job—champagne, good clothes, restaurants and presents for his girlfriend. "My mother would prefer for me to go to university, but I'd rather do this for another five or six years and save a lot."

"Gorbachev is much better for the black market than Brezhnev," Yuri told me. "At least I don't have to worry about getting executed. But you can't do this forever," said Yuri as four police officers clad in greatcoats, unable to understand a word of what we were saying, sat down at the next table.

"There is still a chance of a long jail sentence. I really don't like my profession. There are just too many risks. My plan is to make about 1 million rubles and then leave the country," said Yuri. "But I'm not sure I can do it." He joked, "My wife isn't sure she wants to leave this socialist paradise."

Soviet government poster deriding black market

After we left the café, Maxim reached into his pocket and pulled out a lacquer box. "It's done by a great artist," he assured me as I walked toward the Ethnographic Museum. "You can have it for $30."

11

The Swiss Cheese of Birth Control

One morning I called for a cab at my Leningrad Hotel and gave the driver written instructions in Russian to Children's Hospital #1. Fifteen minutes later, about the time we should have been pulling up to the medical center, I realized the driver was going the wrong way. After much insistence he finally pulled over near the Rimsky-Korsakov Memorial House where a good samaritan helped me explain the mistake to the cabby. Instead of merely turning around he began making a slow loop around the east side of the city headed along the Neva river, passed the Alexander Nevsky Monastery and then swung back in the general direction of the hospital. After pulling into a muddy gas station that looked like something out of the Wild West, complete with broken window panes and rusting pumps, we began to make a long arc around the city. Pausing at one point to pick up a Russian passenger and detour to his destination, the driver finally began making his way across the west side of Leningrad through a forest of Stalinist modern highrises toward the hospital. By the time this 90-minute tour was over there could be no doubt I'd been had. What should have been a two ruble cab ride was now up to 10 rubles. I'd been gouged and the driver headed off with his booty, about $1.67.

Given the depressed value of the ruble, it's hard for even the canniest Russian to get the upper hand in a deal with foreigners. The ruble is such a depressed currency that few foreign enterprises, with the notable exception of McDonald's, will even trade for it.

Instead the Soviets simply barter commodities for sought-after foreign goods. A case in point is tampons, a badly needed product now manufactured in a new Ukrainian joint venture. The Russians get the tampons and the American partner is paid in high quality Georgian cotton that can be used to make the product and sold on the world market. Another high priority is the imported condom which is being bartered for Russian aluminum.

It was Lizbeth Hasse, a young California attorney on the Heart to Heart mission in Leningrad who taught me the facts of life about Soviet condoms. With ten visits to the Soviet Union in the past two years, Hasse was clearly the team's leading business consultant. With offices in San Francisco, Berkeley and Paris, a laptop computer and a modem she had carved out a niche for herself negotiating foreign deals for the Soviet Filmmakers Union, Latvian screenwriters, and performers like Natalya Nogoda, the Soviet actress best known for her performance in *Little Vera*. At the same time she has helped set up Spacebridge, a U.S.–Soviet television program focused on environmental issues as well as the filming of the Heart to Heart project.

When all else failed it was Hasse who knew how to beat the system. Before departing California for Leningrad, Heart to Heart had booked me a hotel reservation for a side trip to Moscow. But when I reached Leningrad, Heart to Heart's director, Jo Ann McGowan, explained that Intourist, the Soviet tour operator, had demanded an astounding $230 a night plus $160 for the roundtrip trainfare. "Of course we canceled for you," McGowan explained. "Don't worry—Liz has a friend who will take care of everything." With Hasse's help I was able to arrange for a hotel, car, driver, meals and a translator in Moscow for several days for less than the cost of a single hotel night at the Intourist rate. And that $160 train ticket to Leningrad wound up costing $18 for a roundtrip first-class berth complete with jazz and classical music. In a country where you can wait a year for your landlord to replace a broken commode, Hasse was a master at getting things done. With a single call she could find a gifted translator to set up ten of the most informative interviews a writer could hope for. From honest taxi drivers to satellite phone calls to a table at the best private restaurant in Moscow, it was Hasse who knew all the tricks. For example, in the spring of 1990, a few months after the pediatric operations in Leningrad, she and Heart to Heart's McGowan flew to an international medical equipment manufacturers convention in Moscow and talked the vendors into donating $1 million worth of state-of-the-art products to the cardiac surgery program in Leningrad.

Given this track record, it was hardly surprising that an Oakland condom firm, Mayer Laboratories, would turn to medical diplomat Hasse in their hour of need. Early in 1990 the Soviet health ministry called on this firm to upgrade the nation's shoddy prophylactics, known as the Swiss cheese of birth control. Officially the Soviet Union annually makes about 100 million condoms, colloquially called "galoshes," for a country of nearly 300 million. Due to unexplained shrinkage, many of these prophylactics never make it to the market. As a result it's often hard to find them in pharmacies. This fact, combined with the unreliability of the condoms that do get to market, helps explain why the Soviet Union has 112 abortions per 1,000 women annually, compared to 28 per 1,000 in our country.

The situation is so serious that according to Francine Gray in *Soviet Women* it is not uncommon for women here to have 10, 12 or more abortions in their lifetime. The situation is so critical that many Americans bring their Russian friends Western condoms as a housewarming present. Black marketeers find this Western product is right up there with running shoes and Levi's, commanding as much as $12 to $15 dollars apiece. Understandably, at this high price the imported condom is frequently reused.

In her hotel room Hasse told me the condom is the only alternative to the rhythm method in a country that lacks other forms of birth control. "Oral contraceptives are nonexistent," she explained. "So are other popular methods. For example, when a Soviet ballet troupe visited San Francisco all 35 ballerinas made special doctor's appointments so they could be fitted with a diaphragm."

Mayer Labs, the official supplier of condoms to the Goodwill Games in Seattle, is no stranger to the international market. And in the Soviet Union their work is especially urgent. Eager to improve birth control and speed the fight against AIDS, the Soviet Health Ministry has made upgrading the condom a high priority. During her visit Hasse worked on Mayer Labs' two-step plan to improve Soviet birth control. First the company will import Japanese "Kimono" brand condoms. "Forget the jokes about them being too small," says Hasse. "One size fits all. These are great condoms." The second phase centers around construction of a $9 million condom factory in Leningrad. The heart of this plan is a state-of-the-art Japanese condom machine. "It takes a while to get this equipment up to speed," she explains. "You have to cure the latex until you get it just right. It's kind of like making fine wine."

Although 3,500 foreign joint ventures are currently waiting for Soviet approval, Hasse has been promised by the health ministry that the Mayer Labs plan will be given priority status. "The catch is we have to find a dependable supply of aluminum to trade for the condoms. There is plenty of aluminum in this country. The only difficulty is that the Soviet's don't have a list of available resources. Each time you go out to do a barter deal you have to start from scratch.

"Part of the problem with bartering in this country is that some Soviets have unrealistic expectations. For example take the foreign businessman working in Estonia who had his own Volvo. It's a great car, but unfortunately parts are hard to come by in Estonia. Luckily he found a parts supplier who was willing to swap Volvo equipment for imported tropical fish. But when the businessman brought in the fish the parts supplier was furious—he claimed that the airport metal detector had sterilized the fish." The publicity over Hasse's work with the condom factory has also brought her calls from other potential clients who don't understand the overseas market. Among those she has rejected outright was the man who called eager to barter "wood products and puppies. I thought his idea was lost in the translation. But that's what he wanted to sell, little dogs."

Although Hasse gets high marks for her efficiency, she feels endlessly frustrated in some of her dealings. "I've had my share of dealing with unreasonable governments. I know about French authorities and their 'pas possible.' I've dealt with the unreasonableness of the IRS and ridiculous post-colonial West African administrators. But all that pales compared to the complexity of doing a deal here. The difficulty is that many of the people you are dealing with have never been to a business meeting, they have never done a contract or a barter deal. In a way that's an advantage because they take the contract you suggest as a model, a template for future dealings. The catch is that you have to do everything in person. The phones and Fax often don't work. Telex is frightfully expensive. On top of that they are used to a long series of foreign business people who come, find out they can't make a killing, and then never come back. I find that the only way to get something done is to come back and work with them in person."

Another problem she explained one day while we were waiting to watch an operation at Children's Hospital #1, is political uncertainty in the business community. "You see in the Soviet Union people have traditionally had their own life and the life their government wanted them to have. Perestroika has opened new possibilities but it has also made life more complicated," she says. For one thing someone who opens an independent cooperative that competes successfully with an established government-owned business is threatening other people's livelihoods. It's not unusual for successful entrepreneurs or restaurant owners to find themselves under attack by jealous competitors.

"And don't forget," Hasse told me, "this is a country with a long tradition of changing the rules in midstream." An arbitrary change, such as Stalin's ban on the teaching of genetics, can quickly turn the norm into a liability. "The Soviets," she explains, "are used to the fact that people with high visibility have been the first ones killed when there was a change of command. As a result people will form a company or cooperative, carry out a business plan and then disband. Prominence in the business world can be a liability. That's why people here are reluctant to give themselves a history.

"At the same time there are some definite advantages to the Soviet system at this point. Democracy in action creates a whole new world for the business community. The trick is to not be the Ugly American. You have to go slowly and not try to drive too hard a bargain. As long as you are comfortable with the idea that you are not going to strike it rich in the Soviet Union, that you may make very little money in any deal, you can succeed. And, of course, once you get a venture in place you're likely to have a monopoly. It's so hard to get a new joint venture started that it's unlikely another foreign firm is going to crowd you."

Hasse, who worked late into the night working out deals with Soviet filmmakers, told me it's easy to be embarrassed in Communist business circles. "They have so little and they give everything away. Here's a county where food is hard to come by and they still throw these lavish parties with delicacies people have obviously been saving for months or found in shops that might be 20 or 30 miles out of town. Paying them back is impossible. A Moscow professor friend of mine got tenure and I wanted to surprise him with a cake and a bottle of champagne." It was here that even Hasse, with all her experience in beating the Soviet system, met her match. As she explained in dismay: "Bakeries are one thing you can count on in the Soviet Union, they are decently stocked. But after standing in a long line for a cake, I found the Russians behind me screaming that this rich foreigner was taking food from their mouths." After giving up in frustration, she walked down the street to one of Moscow's Beriozkas, a hard-currency store well stocked with champagne. But when she arrived at the counter, the clerk took one look at deal-maker Hasse's passport and turned her away. "This store is only for diplomats."

12
The Empire Has No Clothes

One afternoon in Leningrad a Soviet economist told me a story about a Romanian farmer who owned a pig that gave birth to two piglets. The proud man reported to the chairman of the village agricultural committee that his pig had just delivered six piglets. The chairman told the district superintendent for agriculture that the pig had given birth to an even dozen. "Fine," said the superintendent, "we'll just take two and he can keep the rest."

There's more here than just a joke about how one farmer's exaggeration cost him up the bureaucratic ladder. Like Potemkin, Catherine the Great's minister who built village facades to convince the empress that everything was hunky-dory in the provinces, leaders of the withering Communist empire often have difficulty getting at the truth. The Potemkin Village theory of political science lulled the Romanovs into complacency that cost them dearly. In much the same way it made it impossible for the Soviet bureaucracy to deliver on the rich promise of Marx and Lenin. And that is costing the Communist leadership of the 1990s, as well.

One of the most unusual places I visited in Leningrad, the Museum of Religion and Atheism, spoke to one of the prime articles (and fallacies) of the Communist Faith. Natasha Vassilieva, a political science professor and friend of the Oakland doctors I'd joined on their medical mission to this city of 5 million, was my guide. Like many Communists, she had joined the party out of necessity to pursue her chosen profession. We had walked that snowy afternoon through the Peter and Paul Fortress founded by Peter the Great and later used by the Bolsheviks for their decisive attack on the Winter Palace in 1917. Then we made our way across the Neva River to the museum. Of the many Communists I met on my trip, Vassilieva was a favorite. Like a lot of Russians, she could be profound and droll in the same sentence. "Lenin was a brilliant theoretician and a good politician. But the Bolshevik slogan 'land to the peasants, plants to the workers and all power to the Soviets turned out not to be prophetic.' After more than 70 years the peasants have no land, the workers have no plants and Soviets have no power.

"Even Lenin realized during the last years of his life that it was necessary to bring back private enterprise and foreign investment to rescue the Soviet economy. That was why he introduced an antecedent of perestroika in 1921 called the New Economic Policy. My father told me it was an amazing period, suddenly the shops were full again as capitalists rushed in from abroad to fill the shelves. But some of his former allies were horrified by the reintroduction of capitalism. A few even committed suicide. In 1924, after Lenin's death, his successors ended this experiment that could have helped our economy greatly. Today Gorbachev is trying to change things. But there is no economic theory of perestroika. That's why perestroika is in so much trouble."

Heading down the Nevsky Prospekt, we approached the Kazan Cathedral, the city's religious centerpiece framed by 96 perfectly proportioned Corinthian columns. Inside the domed church were bas-relief Biblical art, the icon of the Virgin of Kazan, and a crypt with the heart of Field Marshal Kutuzov, who led the Russian armies in 1812. In 1932 the church was evicted and the government turned this landmark into the Museum of Religion and Atheism. Each day multilingual guides lead visitors through what is surely one of the world's most insulting exhibitions of anti-religious propaganda. Major faiths—Jews, Muslims, Christians—are ridiculed and blasphemed by such exhibits such as a torture chamber used in the Spanish inquisition.

"You can't imagine how much these displays upset many Russian people," Vassilieva told me as we walked with a young couple pushing a stroller past the sacred Torah. Pausing in front of a

"The peasants have no land, the workers have no plants
and Soviets have no power." —Natasha Vassilieva

section featuring paintings of peasant uprisings against the church, she told me: "The Russians are a very religious people, and the state's destruction of the church is bitterly resented."

"Where's the atheism section?" I asked after we'd finished touring this gallery of bigotry. "There isn't one," she told me as we looked up at the great Kazan dome.

Later I examined more hate literature making fun of a black-marketeer trading religious icons for blue jeans. In another hideous cartoon a priest sprinkled holy water on ailing parishioners. In the next panel the same cleric was shown heading into a hospital seeking treatment for a dreadful ailment God had failed to cure. In trying to substitute scientific rationalism for blind faith, the Communists had built something far more fragile than one of Potemkin's villages. God is a hard act to follow. In denying a nation its own faith, by tearing down churches and synagogues, persecuting the religious and even refusing to print their Bibles, the Communist Party became the only place the people could turn to in time of need. The party built itself as the ultimate truth and then failed to deliver.

Like governments everywhere, the Communists didn't have all the answers. Perhaps no one should have expected them to. But they advertised themselves as being the solution to everything, and ironically are in trouble now because the people believed in them.

All health care systems, for example, have their problems. Soaring costs and rising infant mortality are just two of the problems afflicting care in the United States. But the inadequacies dig deeper in the Soviet Union where medical teams operate in the midst of blind government neglect. To make up for a lack of staffing the Soviet nurses came out in their high heels and spent an entire day unloading a truck full of American medical equipment on the icy, unsalted driveway of the Leningrad hospital. And a number of the Soviet intensive care doctors seemed to pride themselves on round the clock shifts, seldom seeing their own apartments.

One night at a reception for our group at the home of American Consul General Richard Miles, I asked a Soviet television reporter why the California team had become a household word in that nation's media. "You have to understand the level of frustration with our medical system. It is the one thing that unites people all

After the Revolution, Lenin Museum, Prague

across our country against the government. People are tired of being lied to, they are tired of being told it's too late or there's nothing that can be done particularly when it involves children. We know we can do better and this heart surgery program proves it."

It is easy to paint a grim picture of the Soviet Union. Indeed, as I interviewed patients, parents and administrators, the word began to filter back that perhaps I was scaring the Russians by being too negative. Eager not to scare anyone off I prefaced an interview with one of the patient's mother this way: "I come from a country that has a lot of problems just as you do you in your country."

The student translator helping me out refused to turn my English into Russian. "What are you talking about?" she shouted at me. "You're visiting a country where 85 percent of the people are classified as poor." I insisted that she translate our conversation, and when she did, both she and the sick child's mother laughed hysterically.

Economic conditions, as well as envy over the new-found freedom of the Eastern European satellites, was sparking new protests across the far-flung union. In early February 1990, when opposition forces scheduled a Sunday pro-democracy demonstration in Moscow, the Kremlin fought back with two extraordinary pieces of television programming. To keep protestors at home, Soviet TV offered prime-time skin flicks and a phone-in lottery show. Among the prizes were banned 19th-century history books. More than 200,000 protestors skipped these tempting shows and filled Red Square for a historic demonstration. And on the day I arrived by train in Moscow there were rumors that Gorbachev was ready to respond directly to the popular will. He did exactly that, announcing that he was ready to abandon the Communist Party monopoly and allow other parties to run slates in democratic elections.

At sundown a French reporter was primping in front of the Kremlin walls as his TV crew finished their setup. And over at the Associated Press a correspondent told me this was probably the biggest political story of the year. But while the American media hailed this historic news, reaction in the streets of Moscow was mixed, a far cry from the exuberant celebrations that greeted similar news in Prague and Berlin a few months earlier. Elena Razlogov, a 16-year-old history student at Moscow University, voiced the popular view that the decision was the inevitable response to the anti-Communist revolts sweeping the world. "People are quitting the Communist Party in droves. Many are people like my own father who joined when he was a young man because it was the only way he could get an important job. Now my younger sister doesn't have to parrot what her teacher thinks. She can say what she wants in class."

At his synagogue office, Moscow's chief Rabbi, Adolf Sheyvich, also praised Gorbachev. He told me, "All people of the Soviet Union suffered greatly during the period of religious intolerance. The Communists now know that the spiritual nature of the Russian people can never be demolished. We have a long way to go but at least we have a leader who has ended the government's anti-religious campaign."

Across town at the Eye Microsurgery Institute, Tanya Kozhevnikova, a secretary, told me the announcement was "inevitable. Gorbachev has no other choice. Communist policies, such as equal pay for workers in similar jobs, have been a failure. New ideas, such as paying more to people who work harder, need to

The Kremlin

be accepted. The only way to push such charges is to have a broader political debate—one that gives more parties a chance."

At Moscow Public School #45 tenth-grader Sergey Plakida was somewhat less optimistic about the prospect of free elections in the Soviet Union, elections that, in theory, could end the Communist monopoly. "In Poland it took the intelligentsia and the working class to change the government. It was mostly intelligentsia at the big Moscow pro-democracy demonstration. Only when they are joined by the working class can you expect there to be a real challenge to the Communist party. People here have lived with the Communist idea all their life. It has become almost a religion. But our lack of a democratic history makes us vulnerable. The Communists know that if you repeat the same idea, however wrong, enough times, a lot of people will believe you.

"This is not going to be another Poland or Hungary. Gorbachev is using his triumphs in foreign relations, an area where he has done good things, to bolster the Communists domestically where things are not so good. I think the speed of change depends on political development. Unfortunately we have the lowest level of political development in the socialist world. We are like Romania and Albania."

Reading Gorbachev's speech aloud from *Pravda*, my friend Alex Harruczinov was also cautionary: "I appreciate the idea of reform. We were taught in schools that the Americans were waiting for the Communists to come and save them. That turned out to be wrong. Now we know the Communists can't even save our own country. I can't believe that the party will be open to transplanting democracy into the corpse of socialism. They have put so many obstacles in the way of a real political transformation."

Despite his pessimism Alex and I decided to celebrate the big news from the Kremlin at the Cosmos Hotel smorgasbord. Unfortunately we couldn't get into the Cosmos because we'd left our passports in the car, now locked by our driver who had headed off for his own dinner. We compromised by heading across the street to a hard-currency-only hamburger stand. We toasted the revolution with cheeseburgers and Cokes paid for in dollars. An hour later, after a quick stop at a bookstore to pick up some perestroika literature, he dropped me off at my hotel, the Rossiya. "Don't worry about those cockroaches in your room," he said with a grin as we embraced and he handed me a small present. "I tell all my visiting friends to just look upon them as pets."

Back in Leningrad the following day I made an evening visit to the city's Hyde Park corner outside the Kazan Church where every night non-Communist political organizers met to argue and debate their future. Because no seating was available at coffee shops on a Friday night in the heart of Dostoyevsky's storied city, I sat with Vladimir, a warehouseman, and Maxim, a carpenter, on a cold park bench facing the Religion of Museum of Religion and Atheism. A lunar eclipse had just begun over Leningrad as we discussed the difficulty of trying to overturn the Communist monopoly. "Now they are promising sausages in the shops," Vladimir told me. "But the government is still not promising basic reforms."

Maxim agreed: "Our problem is that since 1917 we have lost everything of consequence, even the religion which is the basis of our culture. We've had 72 years of socialism, which means our people have forgotten what it's like to live in a civilized state."

Exploring Peter the Great's Imperial Palace at Petrodvorets west of Leningrad on the Gulf of Finland the next day, I heard something that made me think Vladimir and Maxim both underestimated the Soviets' potential for rapid political change. That afternoon, Natasha Chazova, one of the student translators at the children's hospital, was showing me around the Versailles-like world of the Romanovs in her beloved hometown. As we walked through the Imperial Gardens in a snowstorm, she mentioned a recent trip she'd taken to Bulgaria with a classmate. "Things just seemed better there, even the food." The notion that the Soviet Union is falling behind the weakest of its former satellites suggests just how vulnerable the Communists have become.

Something else Chazova told me struck a chord about my confidence in the Russian people. Standing on a bus bound for the railway station and my train back to Leningrad, she mentioned, almost casually, the aggressive way Bulgarian men pursued Russian women during her visit. We kicked around several possible explanations, and then finally I suggested, "Perhaps it's because the Russian women are very beautiful." "Do you think so?" she asked. "Yes," I told her, "and the men are very handsome."

Many times during my visit, the Russians, particularly the men, had asked, "How do we look to you, do we seem nervous or unhappy?" My answer was always no—and I meant it. The Russians were, to my mind, the beautiful people, poised, articulate, funny, unfailingly generous and always good company. They also, it seemed to me, were very smart and rather canny. Given half a chance and a little help I have no doubt they can persevere in their current era of change and build something much better for themselves and their children.

The next morning, when my plane took off and banked over Leningrad, two pieces of good news were on my mind. The Soviet government, in the interest of equal time, had decided to shut down the Museum of Religion and Atheism on Sunday mornings to let the Orthodox Church resume holding services after a 48-year hiatus. And at Leningrad Children's Hospital #1, by the time my flight reached San Francisco the following day, Russian surgeons—thanks to the tutelage of the Oakland doctors—would be doing their first shunts and bands on Soviet children who had been "inoperable" just two weeks earlier.

Old Town Hall Clock, Prague

Conclusion

Revolution creates unique opportunities. Among them is a chance to learn from the mistakes of past leaders who succumbed to the myth of invincibility in their own revolution. Did the Communists fail to heed these lesson? Was Communism doomed from the start? Was the concept a sound one buried beneath the weight of the bureaucracy? Or did Lenin's political heirs simply lack the intelligence and imagination necessary to make good on the rich promise of the October Revolution when a mere 28,000 Bolsheviks took over a country of 150 million.

It is tempting to pass judgment, to suggest that one of these factors, a combination of them or something altogether different is behind the stunningly rapid disintegration of the Communist way of life in Eastern Europe and the Soviet Union. But my purpose in these chapters instead has been to let the facts speak for themselves, to show what life has been like for these people and how they are trying to change it. The one conclusion I draw is this: For every person who flourished under Communism, there were millions who did not. The sheer weight of the arithmetic undercut the rich promise of socialism until people's hope simply gave out. And one strong conviction I hope emerges from this book is that a small band of goodwill ambassadors from the Bay Area, equipped with medical knowledge instead of a nuclear arsenal, was able to do more to bring a sense of unity and comradeship with this one-time "evil empire" than any summit could ever hope to.

I would add a note of caution to those ready to chortle over the demise of Communism without the West having to fire a shot. Remember that this courtship with democracy is by no means certain to emerge into long-lasting marital bliss. The Communists may be battered, but they are not knocked out. Even in the twilight of the Communist regime in Poland, I saw party faithful weeping at the end of an era that had brought the privileged *nomenklatura* an enviable way of life. In the Soviet Union, I heard voices, strange as it may seem, arguing that Stalin, for all his faults, at least brought law and order to a dissolute nation. The Communists justified their purges on the theory that "you have to break a few eggs to make an omelette." Lest anyone doubt whether hard-liners in the Soviet Union are willing to assert themselves, I would suggest asking the people in China what they think.

No one knows what will evolve in the Iron Curtain countries as they move toward capitalism, with its rewards but also its harsh realities. As Sarah Miles, wife of the American consul general in Leningrad, told me one night: "Anyone who predicts what is going

St. George's Hospital, Leipzig—the first protest in 777 years

Palace Square, cradle of the Russian Revolution, Leningrad

to happen in the next year, let alone the next month, is just guessing." Who can predict the results when state-owned industries are forced to go it alone in a free-enterprise system? Will the workers in Poland, East Germany and other former satellite countries react to unemployment, which is almost guaranteed in some major industries? What if rampant inflation occurs? Will these economies be able to compete on the world market? Will the new breed of leaders get caught up in the myth of invincibility? As a sobering reminder of what can happen, we need only recall recent history, when the German people, out of a sense of economic and social despair, embraced an unknown Adolf Hitler to lead them to salvation.

Even now, in the 1990 revolution, the Germans present a fascinating case study. The people of East Germany face a more formidable transition than any of their compatriots in the grip of revolutionary change. As they feel their way into the sunlight of freedom, they do so under the cloud of political, economic and social reunification with West Germany, testing not only their resolve but also requiring two unheard-of commodities— enlightenment and goodwill—from superpowers over whom they have no control.

I remember driving north one day over the border from Czechoslovakia and running smack into a demonstration in Leipzig, the protest capital of East Germany. The entire staff of St. George's Hospital was on the picket line blocking traffic during their lunch hour. This was the first demonstration in the history of this 777-year-old medical center. Doctors, nurses, administrators and staff were all standing side by side, demanding relief from Communist austerity. Nurses being pushed about in wheelchairs carried picket signs as doctors marched with huge banners.

Head nurse Barbara Seidel told me the facility was so short of bed space that elective surgeries were now being postponed half a year or longer. "We've had a new surgery wing under construction since 1981," she complained, "and it's still not finished. We're lacking basic supplies ranging from syringes and gloves to stationery." Hospital Director Rudolf Weiner added that he has lost more than 30 doctors and 230 staff over the past two years. "Why shouldn't they move to West Germany? Here a doctor makes $75 a month. There they can earn $4,000 a month."

The demonstration stopping traffic outside St. George's Hospital was merely an extension of the staff's participation in Leipzig's regular Monday night protests in the Town Square. Those demonstrations, which began in October 1989, routinely attracted 150,000 to 200,000 people and were instrumental in bringing down East Germany's Honecker government. "Now we are trying to make sure the Communists are pushed out of power forever," he told me. "It seemed logical for us to extend our protest to the workplace. We are tired of waiting for our new wing to be finished. We are tired of waiting for apartments. We are tired of waiting 10 to 13 years for a new car that's made out of plastic. We are just plain tired."

Later that day I drove to the heart of this city of 700,000, eager to visit St. Nikolai Church, the birthplace of the Leipzig peace prayers. More than four centuries ago Martin Luther's reformation began in this city. Leipzig's new reformation began in the fall of 1989, just a few blocks from the site where Luther

"We are tired of waiting for our new wing to be finished."
—Dr. Rudolph Weiner

changed religious history. Christian Weber, a seminary student, told me how a small group of prayer meetings at St. Nikolai spawned demonstrations that ultimately transformed the East German government.

Initially, the church provided meeting space for dissidents eager to meet and talk about fleeing their country via Budapest and Vienna. But by early September a broader protest group began to assemble for the Monday night peace prayers. Within weeks an overflow crowd was flocking to the church planning political action. "Some church elders felt St. Nikolai should only be open to church members," Weber said. "But ultimately it was decided that the sanctuary would welcome non-Christians. The final decision was to simply be for the people and let them use the church for political organizing. We didn't send anyone away."

By early October new opposition parties, including the Social Democrats, the Green Party and the Human Rights Party, were beginning to organize in this political sanctuary created by the church. Eager to thwart these protests, state security forces and Communist Party members arrived early on October 9, filling St. Nikolai in the hope that they could prevent regulars from attending the peace prayers. The minister welcomed the Communists with a warm Shalom and a call for dialogue. By mid-October the peace prayers had grown into mass demonstrations with more than 150,000 protestors calling for democracy. These demonstrations and similar protests around the country provided the political muscle necessary to bring down the old regime without a single shot being fired.

Like the rest of Eastern Europe and the Soviet Union, the East Germans find themselves in the midst of one of history's most complex and fascinating political transitions. Has any government ever brought a larger dowry to a political wedding than the West Germans? Can democracy answer the prayers of Dr. Weiner and his staff at St. George's?

I believe the denouement will likely be every bit as surprising as the revolution that is changing the map of Europe and even the Soviet Union. From reunification in Germany to breakaway republics in Mother Russia, this is history written with ink likely to take a long time to dry. What I've seen and heard persuades me that we are fortunate indeed that these new revolutionaries at least learned enough about Communism to know how to overthrow it. Clearly they have mastered Trotsky's teaching: "...The mere existence of privations is not enough to cause an insurrection. If it were, the masses would always be in revolt. It is necessary that the bankruptcy of the social regime, being conclusively revealed, should make these privations intolerable, and that new conditions and new ideas should open the prospects of a revolutionary way out."

Afterword:
Surfing on a Deluge

Theory is not a note which you can present at any moment to reality for payment. If a theory proves mistaken we must revise it or fill out its gaps. We must not wander in the dark, repeating ritual phrases, useful for the prestige of the leaders, but which nevertheless slap the living reality in the face. —Leon Trotsky

I didn't know anyone read Marxism anymore," said the Panasonic cellular phone sales manager next to me in seat 3B as we took off from Dallas on a flight to San Francisco one afternoon in the fall of 1990. I was tempted to begin explaining why, in the months after my trip to Eastern Europe and the Soviet Union, I had taken such a deep interest in the works of theorists like Marx, Engels, Lenin, Trotsky and Gorbachev. But before I could get started he began filling me in on the challenges of working for a Japanese company. "As they say in Tokyo, 'The beatings will continue until morale improves.'"

"Stalinism lives," I told him, as the steward arrived with our drinks.

In the waning days of 1990 it seemed impossible to stop thinking about what had gone so horribly wrong in the Communist world. As the Soviet Union began to resemble the world's largest Outward Bound school, a society that tested the survival skills of its people every day, it was tempting to look back to people like Trotsky, who, a few years before his assassination in Mexico, attempted to lay the blame at the feet of bureaucracy:

"The basis of bureaucratic rule is the poverty of society in objects of consumption, with the resulting struggle of each against all. ... When there is little goods, the purchasers are compelled to stand in line. When the lines are very long, it is necessary to appoint a policeman to keep order.

Such is the starting point of the power of the Soviet bureaucracy. It 'knows' who is to get something and who has to wait."

A couple days before Thanksgiving in the midst of what commentators were beginning to call Gorbachev's "November crisis," I made an appointment to visit with the Russian historian Martin Malia, author of a penetrating analysis of the Communist crisis, "To the Stalin Mausoleum." Published under the pseudonym "Z" in the winter 1990 issue of *Daedalus*, he focused on the historical inevitability of the fall of communism in the Soviet Union. Scholars on both sides of the Atlantic were fascinated by this fresh viewpoint, which was excerpted by the *New York Times*. Malia had begun writing shortly before the Berlin Wall fell, before "the collapse of Central European communism... demonstrated that Leninist regimes are mortal." His thrust was that "because of structural reasons going back to 1917, communism was irreformable; it could only be wholly dismantled if the nations it had ruined were to survive." For Malia believed that Gorbachev's reforms only delayed the collapse of the Soviet empire. He urged the West to help ease the crisis by speeding up arms control and providing economic aid to the Soviet private sector.

Waiting for "Z" to arrive at his Dwinelle Hall office at the University of California in Berkeley, I read news of Gorbachev's historic Paris arms control conference with George Bush and leaders of 20 other nations. "What a long way the world has come!" the Russian leader said after the officials signed treaties that would destroy armaments by the tens of thousands. In just a couple weeks Gorbachev would be off to Oslo to accept the Nobel Peace Prize. The Cold War was finally over.

Although Malia conceded that Gorbachev "might be agile enough to become his own successor," he believed it was probably impossible for the President to effectively lead his country out of the wilderness after a 73-year regime that has stretched from Bolshevism to perestroika. "The Communists are surfing on a deluge," said the historian. "Communist doctrine had always held that the conquests of socialism were irreversible. But the struggle against the system within Eastern Europe showed that the conquest could be reversed over an enormous area. This turned out to be a loss of legitimacy for Communists everywhere, including Russia. Now perestroika is over and communism is over. You've got to proceed with steps to liquidate the system, not to patch it up. That's the essential thing."

Malia, just back from the Soviet Union, said the quality of life had deteriorated in recent months. "Russia is in worse shape than the satellites. They've had communism for much longer. They've left behind a much bigger establishment. The physical plant is more decayed. The population is less willing to embrace the risks of marketization, except in the Baltics or the western Ukraine."

Couldn't the Soviets follow the lead of their former satellites?

"I find it very difficult to imagine a scenario for a successful transition," he said. "It's difficult enough to imagine it in countries like Poland and Czechoslovakia that at least have a memory of democracy earlier in this century. In East Germany we can see it because they were absorbed by an existing market economy. But it would be extraordinarily difficult to do this in the Soviet Union. The Soviet government thought of imitating the Polish example, but they discovered they didn't have the popular support. The population wouldn't trust them through all the hardships that a shock therapy program would necessitate.

"It's unrealistic to expect that someone as indecisive as Gorbachev, who has thrown away chance after chance to use the new powers he has been given since he was elected president in March, 1990, will do something positive with the economy. I can't see him breaking up the industrial ministries, auctioning off state property, giving away land to the farmers, or doing something drastic to break the logjam."

Malia's grim assessment reminded me of some of the people I'd met on my own visit. At a drugstore in a small town near Leningrad, the pharmacist had given me a list of common medications that were out of stock, such as the heart medicine, digitalis. "There are almost no medicines left in the country," he warned, "a fact that creates a chance of epidemics. There is now a danger of mass migration to the West, leading to turbulence and disorder. We will have to support rebuilding this country to keep things stationary, but this is going to be staggeringly difficult. The whole physical plant probably has to be replaced. This is going to be a process of years and decades. There isn't going to be any peace dividend."

Malia doubted the Soviet army would stage a coup in the midst of this crisis because it's against their tradition and they simply couldn't run an economy. "It could become a government of public safety under Gorbachev. Many Soviets worry he could use the military to jail some of the democrats, to restore order and keep thing minimally supplied. This would be a soft dictatorship. If he does it, I bet George Bush will support him."

Could Gorbachev reach a political compromise that might form a basis for rebuilding this nation?

"It's too late," he said. "The fact is that by September of this year the federal and republican structures of the Soviet Union were effectively dismantled. Incredible. The nation is being reduced to a barter economy, with every man for himself. The drift toward disintegration and localization will continue until it hits bottom. There is no real government in the Soviet Union now, neither a central nor local government."

Malia's assessment raised some important questions about the breakup of a superpower. It appeared there were nearly as many risks for the Soviet Union's allies as there were for its enemies, past and present. "In this atmosphere of political disintegration there is understandable concern among the Soviet people that another nuclear power plant go wrong or tactical nuclear weapons might fall into the wrong hands," he said.

At the very moment the world was worrying about Saddam Hussein creating nuclear power for Baghdad, Malia said the possibility existed that one of the breakaway Soviet republics might suddenly help itself to nuclear weapons. The breakup of a nation covering a sixth of the earth's surface would upset the balance of power from our nation to China. Obviously all of us have a stake in the Soviet Union's peaceful transition to democracy.

Can the Soviets join their brethren in Eastern Europe, where, for example, the East Germans have already scrapped the last of their dangerous nuclear power plants? Perhaps today's frightening possibilities will help the Soviet people reverse the totalitarian history of a nation created by violence rather than consensus. For as the old order breaks apart, they now have a perfect opportunity to create a modern republic that mirrors their true identity.

Malia may be right when he suggests that the job exceeds Gorbachev's grasp. Indeed, given the state of disintegration, a single leader may not be able to hold the nation together at this moment in its history. As long as the bureaucracy remains the power behind the Kremlin, the Soviets are likely to flounder. If it does, relief will probably be delivered from outside the system.

Leaving Malia's office and walking back across the Berkeley campus, I recalled a hopeful moment in Leningrad. When the Heart to Heart team pulled up for its second visit in January, 1990 with a truck carrying $500,000 worth of medical equipment, the entire staff of Leningrad Hospital #1 came out to celebrate. Nurses in their high heels gleefully slid down the icy driveway to help unload. Administrators were right behind them. "You have to understand," a Soviet doctor told the American team. "So many times people come to Russia and promise to help us. Then we never hear from them again. We can't believe you're here again, that you came back."

BIBLIOGRAPHY

Abel, Elie. *Shattered Bloc* (Boston: Houghton Mifflin, 1990)

Aganbegyan, Abel. *Inside Perestroika* (New York: Harper & Row, 1989)

Ash, Timothy Garton. *The Uses of Adversity: Essays on the Fate of Central Europe* (New York: Random House, 1989)

Cracraft, James, ed. *The Soviet Union Today* (Chicago: Bulletin of Atomic Scientists, 1983)

Friedland, William, et al. *Revolutionary Theory* (Totowa, New Jersey: Allanheld, Osmun & Co., 1982)

Goldman, Emma. *My Disillusionment in Russia* (New York: Crowell, 1970)

Gray Francine. *Soviet Women* (New York: Doubleday, 1989)

Hamerow, Theodore. *From the Finland Station* (New York: Basic Books, 1990)

Havel, Vaclav. *Disturbing the Peace* (New York: Knopf, 1990)

Kaiser, Robert. *Russia: The People and the Power* (New York: Atheneum, 1976)

Knaus, William. *Russian Medicine* (Boston: Beacon, 1981)

Mandel, William. *Soviet Women* (New York: Anchor, 1975)

Medvedev, Zhores. *The Legacy of Chernobyl* (New York: Norton, 1990)

Mezhendov, Vladimir. *One Way Ticket to Democracy* (Progess Publishers: Moscow, 1989)

Mills, C. Wright. *The Marxists* (New York: Dell, 1969)

Novosti Press Agency Moscow. *USSR Yearbook '89* (Novosti, 1989)

Plimak, E. *Lenin's Political Testament* (Moscow: Progress Publishers, 1988)

Smith, Hedrick. *The Russians* (New York: Times Books, 1976)

About The Author

The author of books on medicine, California politics, education and nuclear weapons, Roger Rapoport is the travel writer at the *Oakland Tribune*. He has written many national magazine articles for publications like *Parade*, *Esquire*, *Americana*, *California* and *Longevity*, and is the author or co-author of guidebooks to Asia, the Rockies, California and Around the World travel. "I'm either half or three-quarters Russian," he says, "depending on where you stand on the issue of Lithuanian independence." He lives in Berkeley, California with his wife Margot and their children Jonathan and Elizabeth.